ILLUSTRATED LIVES
OF THE
SAINTS

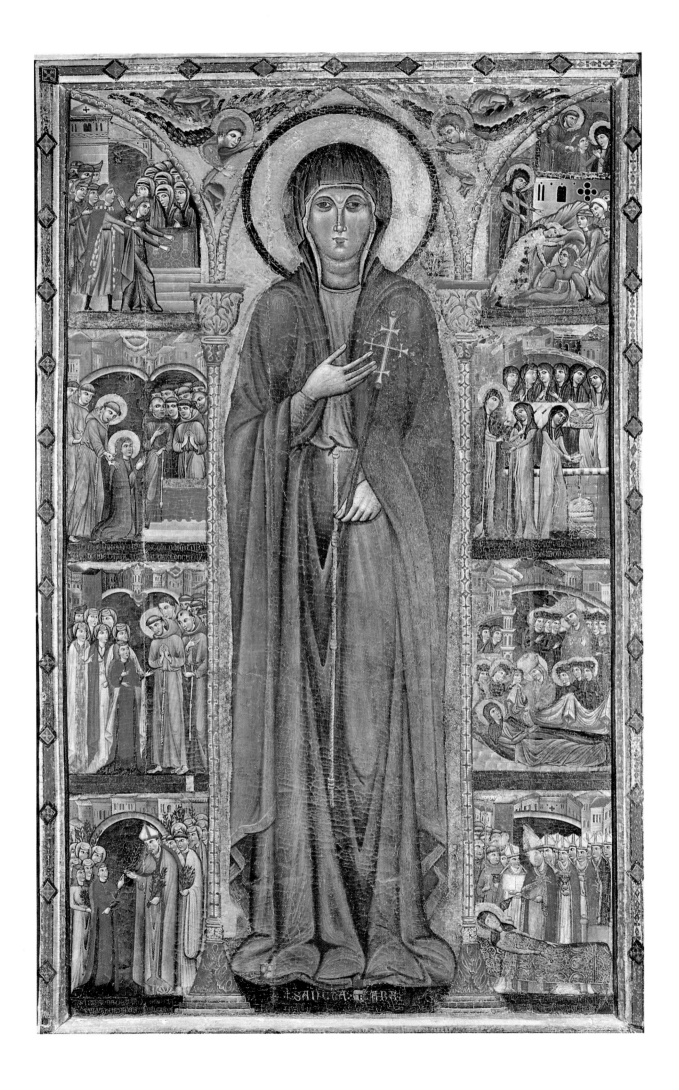

ILLUSTRATED LIVES
OF THE
SAINTS

John McNeill

BISON GROUP

First published in 1995 by
Bison Books Ltd.
Kimbolton House
117a Fulham Road
London SW3 6RL

ISBN 1-85841-190-4

Printed in The Czech Republic

PAGE 1
St. Thomas Aquinas, detail of the Demidoff
altarpiece by Carlo Crivelli, 1476.

PAGE 2
St. Clare, panel painting in the convent of Sta
Chiara, Assisi, *c.*1300, showing the saint with
scenes from her life.

PAGE 3
St. Guthlac sailing to Crowland to establish his
monastic retreat there, from the late twelfth-
century *Guthlac Roll.*

RIGHT
St. George and the Dragon by the nineteenth-
century English painter Sir Edward Poynter.

Contents

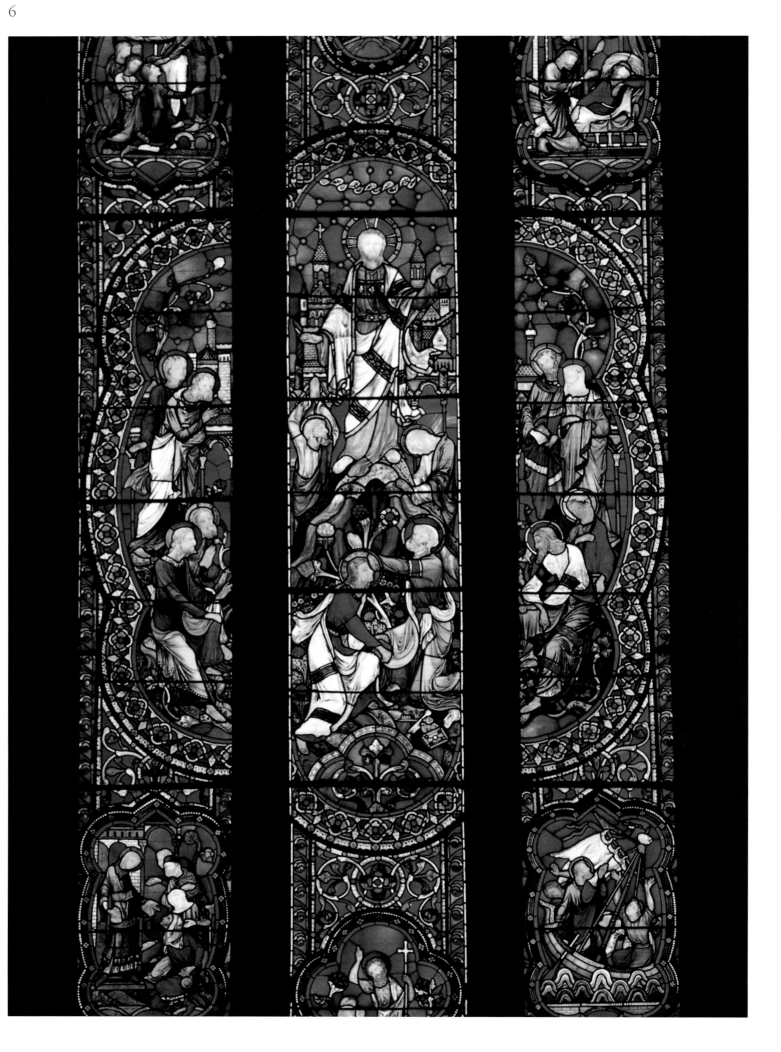

Introduction

Saints occupy a peculiar place in society. In its original usage, the Latin term *sanctus* signified holy, specifically devoted to God, set apart. It might refer to both objects and people, and it did not, at least not until recently, indicate a stainless character or high moral tone, simply a holiness, or sacredness to God. This idea of separateness, of the individual devoting his or her life to God, or being specially favored by Him, invests the saint with what might be described as metaphysical power, with insights into the nature of Being, and supernatural abilities transmitted through the Holy Spirit. Thus saints do not belong to any particular category of society, but rather occupy a place somewhere between this world and God. It is this which gives saints their fascination to the historian of the Middle Ages; they bubble up through the strata of an acutely conventional society, take precedence over popes and kings, becoming rallying points for popular devotion. Above all, they cannot be brought low by persecution, for their martyrdom is the kiss of a new life.

The veneration of saints has an ancient pedigree, and rests on the belief that since the saint is human and, being favored by God, must now be in Heaven, he or she might intercede on behalf of the living. The *Martyrium Polycarpi* of c.156 maintains that Polycarp's disciples held a feast in his honor on the anniversary of his martyrdom. Although the early martyr cults borrowed much from pagan funerary rites, the anniversary they celebrated was not the terrestrial birthday of the deceased, but their arrival in Heaven, i.e. their death. Initially these feasts were celebrated at the grave of the martyr, and were thus purely local, but by the third century one hears of the practice of dismembering the body of the saint so as to distribute relics more widely, and of the enshrinement of secondary relics, such as strips of cloth, which had been in contact with the body of the martyr. By this date Christians also began to travel to visit the shrines of martyrs, or those places in the Holy Land associated with the life of Christ. Helena, Constantine's mother, undertook a pilgrimage to Bethlehem and Jerusalem in 325, and was followed in the late fourth century by Jerome and the Spanish nun Etheria, whose account of her journeys, the *Peregrina-*

tio Etheriae, recounts visits to shrines in Egypt, the Holy Land, Asia Minor and Constantinople.

Virtually all early saints were martyrs, but after Constantine granted the Church a legal identity in the 313 Edict of Milan, the persecutions abated. A second group of saints then began to attract public veneration. To distinguish these figures from the martyrs, they were honored by the term *confessor*, meaning that they bore witness to Christ through their enduring confession of the Christian faith. The great teachers and ascetics were so honored, figures such as Ambrose, Jerome, Simeon Stylites and Martin of Tours, and the distinction between martyr and confessor, while not rigid, seems to have held a meaning for the early Christian communities of Europe. Gregory of Tours, writing in the late sixth century, epitomized this in his composition of two

LEFT: Christ in Heaven surrounded by saints. Hereford Cathedral.

RIGHT: SS Luke and Peter, from a thirteenth-century Salzburg lectionary.

anthologies of saints' lives; the *Glory of the Confessors* and *Glory of the Martyrs*.

The methods whereby an individual might be sainted varied, both historically and geographically, but there are two essentials which indicate an acceptance of sainthood. The first is popular acclaim; any saint must be so called *per viam cultus*, by way of a cult. In the early Church this took the form of a spontaneous outpouring of devotion at the grave, which, if maintained on the anniversary of the death over a number of years, constituted a cult. Subsequently the cult might spread, either through a distribution of relics, or through the dedication of churches and altars to the saint. The second prerequisite is that the name of the saint should be entered in a list, or canon, hence the term canonization. This was usually done locally; by the fourth century bishops began to exercise a loose control over the process by consenting to the celebration of an annual feast in honor of the saint, in other words guaranteeing observation of the anniversary of the saint's death. As Christians began collating local canons to produce more general lists of feasts, local cults began to spread, and a more universal calendar took shape.

The institution of papal canonization is a late development, first encountered in 993, when Pope John XV acclaimed Ulrich of Augsburg a saint and added his name to the *Roman Martyrology*. Thereafter, papal approval was frequently sought as a means of legitimizing new candidates for the rank of sainthood. It was also felt that this offered some sort of protection against the proliferation of false cults, a useful safeguard in an increasingly saint-obsessed early medieval society. Nonetheless, it was not until *c.*1170 that Pope Alexander III decreed that no individual might be venerated as a saint without the approval of the Church of Rome, an initiative which became widely accepted during the papacy of Innocent III (1199-1216). Although intended to prevent abuses, concentrating the process of canonization in Rome made it no less vulnerable to aggressive petitions, or personal whim, and while extremely popular cult figures such as Osmund of Salisbury failed to win papal approval, purely political candidates, such as Edward the Confessor, were sainted. The actual procedures evolved slowly, but by the later Middle Ages the establishment of a papal commission was standard, charged with investigating the life of the candidate. If this was found to be exemplary, the commission would then pass on to consider the reported miracles. This obviously had an impact on the writing of saints' lives, for anxious cathedral chapters would often commission a life of their hoped-for saint from a leading writer, with a view to impressing the papal commission. The life would be presented as without moral stain; and the miracles would carry the names of witnesses. The formal process of canonization was to all intents and purposes a reversal of medieval priorities, for what mattered in the matter of popular devotion were miracles; the life was for inspirational stories.

Before passing on to the main text, a few practical observations should be made. I have included short lives of 100 saints, each entry arranged alphabetically for ease of reference. As the Church has at various times recognized well over 10 000 saints, and sanctions the Feast of All Saints (November 1), in honor of those it has not individually sainted and who are known only to God, this is but a small selection. The criteria adopted in making a choice were neither rigorous nor historical, and they essentially reflect a personal bias. About half of those included might be regarded as Universal Saints, that is to say their cult was widely celebrated in both the Eastern and Western Churches. The other half enjoyed more local cults, and their inclusion was motivated out of a desire for variety, either in terms of the type of cult they generated, or the nature of the lives they led. Wherever possible I have included references to the earliest known source material, and indicated the date at which this might have been written. The illustrations are in many ways the most important element of the book, for taken as a whole they say something about how saints came to be perceived, the miracles they worked, their position in an ecclesiastical hierarchy, and their promise. For saints, like angels, offer a connection between the world of the palpably mundane and the eternity of a world to come.

Without the interest and goodwill of colleagues and friends, this volume would have been impossible to write. I should particularly like to thank the staff of the British Library for their help in locating some of the more obscure source material, and my students for their patient forbearance as I became immersed in a heady mixture of hagiography, pilgrimage, cult imagery and story-telling. That I was even encouraged to do so came as a bonus. Kusuma Barnett, Shirley Liffen and Gale Thomas were extremely generous in their support, and I was touched by the style and sympathy with which they conjured up lives of Olaf, Alban and Catherine. To them I owe a considerable debt. I should also like to single out Malcolm Armstrong, Ian Dunn, Roger Norris, Brian O'Callaghan and Barbara Vossel for the practical and conversational stimulus they offered the book.

The greatest debt is owed to those who taught me to appreciate medieval history and art in the first place. Their ideas and methods permeated any thinking I entertained on the subject of sainthood, and I wish to take this opportunity to thank Joanna Cannon, Eric Fernie, Lindy Grant, Sandy Heslop, Peter Kidson, Andrew Martindale and John Mitchell for their efforts to equip me with a little understanding. The flaws and omissions are entirely mine. Finally, I should like to thank my editor, Jessica Hodge, and picture researcher, Suzanne O'Farrell, for managing the project with such convivial ease. The book is dedicated to Anthony Gibbs, whose inventions could match the finest within these covers.

ABOVE: The Three Magi, from a twelfth-century English psalter.
BELOW LEFT: Seventeenth-century saints' altarpieces in Notre-Dame-des-Cordeliers, Laval, France.
RIGHT: Simeon the Stylite on a sixth-century reliquary.

Aethelwold *c.908-84*
Monk and bishop Feast day August 1

Born at Winchester, Aethelwold was taken into the household of Athelstan, King of Wessex, probably while still quite young. Aethelwold was ordained priest by Aelfheah, Bishop of Winchester, on the same day as **Dunstan**, and between *c.*940 and 954 served as a monk at Glastonbury while Dunstan was abbot. His request to leave Glastonbury to work under the reforming abbot Aymard at Cluny (Burgundy) was refused by King Eadred, and instead, in 954, he was asked to restore the lapsed abbey of Abingdon (Oxfordshire). While there he invited "skilled chanters" from the abbey of Corbie (Picardy) to join the community, and sent Osgar, one of the monks, to study the monastic customs of Fleury (St-Benoît-sur-Loire). These initiatives probably postdated Dunstan's return from exile at St. Peter's, Ghent, in 957, but are the earliest evidence for the adoption of the continental reform in Anglo-Saxon England.

Aethelwold's appointment as Bishop of Winchester in 963 completed the groundwork necessary to ensure the monastic reform took root, for with Oswald in charge of both Worcester and York, and Dunstan at Canterbury, the senior English bishoprics were in the hands of like-minded men. In 964 Aethelwold took the dramatic step of throwing the secular canons out of Winchester Cathedral, replacing them with a congregation of Benedictine monks. Two years later he did the same at the New Minster, Winchester, and followed this up by founding or re-founding the great Fenland abbeys of Peterborough, Ely, Thorney and Crowland. Aethelwold's practical abilities, both as an administrator and as an artist, were remarkable. He is recorded as a cook at Glastonbury, a bell-founder at Abingdon, and a mason at Winchester, and his foundation of a monastic scriptorium at the Old Minster, Winchester, was responsible for the growth of one of the most significant centers of book production in medieval Europe.

Aethelwold's most celebrated achievement was his hosting of the 973 Council of Winchester, in concert with Oswald, Dunstan and King Edgar. The Council was responsible for drawing up the *Regularis Concordia*, a set of liturgical customs which were to be observed in all English monastic houses. In effect the *Regularis* codified the aims of the monastic reform; by describing the offices to be sung on each day of the year, and the principal liturgical areas of the church, and by defining the relations between a monastic chapter and its royal benefactors, it became the backbone of English monastic life for the next century.

Agatha *Third century?*
Virgin and martyr Feast day February 5

The earliest surviving mention of Agatha is in Jerome's *Martyrology*, and the importance of the cult is attested by the foundation of two churches under her dedication in sixth-century Rome and one in sixth-century Ravenna. She is also featured in the Procession of Virgins on the north wall of Sant' Apollinare Nuovo, Ravenna, of *c.*561. The later accounts of her life are pure invention, however. According to these she came from a wealthy Sicilian family, and as a Christian took a vow of virginity. Her beauty attracted the attention of the consul Quintinian, but she rejected him and so in punish-

ABOVE: *Benedictional of St. Aethelwold.* The miniature represents a bishop, possibly Aethelwold himself, pronouncing a blessing. A poem written in gold at the opening of the manuscript states that the Benedictional was made for Aethelwold's own use by Godeman, one of the Winchester monks, and the reference to miracles witnessed at the shrine of St. Swithun in 971 suggests it was written between 971 and Aethelwold's death in 984. The Benedictional consists of a collection of texts used by a bishop when blessing the congregation during the Mass.

ment she was handed over to the strikingly named brothel-keeper, Aphrodisia, who failed to corrupt her. Quintinian then invoked an Imperial edict aimed against Christians and had her tortured, the gruesome ordeals almost matching those inflicted on St. George in their brutality, featuring rods, racks, fire and shears. Finally her breasts were cut off, and she died in prison in Catania of her injuries. This last indignity gave rise to the attribute with which she is most commonly identified in medieval art, a platter on which are displayed her severed breasts.

Alban *Third century?*
Martyr Feast day June 22

Alban is first mentioned in a mid-fifth-century life of Germanus of Auxerre by Constantius, and the story of his martyrdom was recounted by Gildas, in his *De Excidio* of *c.*516-47, and Bede, in his *Historia Ecclesiastica Gentis Anglorum* of *c.*716-31. Both suggest he was martyred in about 305, though modern scholars have argued his death was brought about under Septimus Severus, around 209. Either way, the fact of Alban's martyrdom is not in doubt, and as the earliest British martyr his cult acquired considerable importance during the Middle Ages.

The basic story is related by Bede. According to this, Alban was a Roman citizen living in Verulamium, who gave shelter to a Christian priest fleeing from persecution. Impressed by his faith, Alban converted and, having persuaded the priest to escape, donned his cloak and surrendered himself to the Roman authorities. Once it was realized Alban was not the original target but a respected Roman citizen, he was asked to make a sacrifice to the pagan gods. He refused and was flogged, after which his execution was ordered by the presiding judge. Alban was taken out of the town to the river Ver, but the crowds gathered on the bridge were so great that neither he, nor his captors, were able to cross. It was then that the miracles flowed. First, the river dried up to allow a

ABOVE: *The Martyrdom of St Agatha* by Giambattista Tiepolo.

LEFT: *St. Agatha* by Bernardino Luini. The cult of St. Agatha became particularly popular in post-medieval Italy, where a number of important Carmelite convents took her dedication. Luini's sixteenth-century visualization of the saint shows Agatha wearing a garland of flowers and holding her severed breasts.

i pacnf lad feru du brane lu ere furbiz   H eft mie de fun fair lunges choice

passage, a spectacle which persuaded the executioner to throw down his sword and ask to die with Alban. Second, a spring suddenly appeared out of the hill beyond the river, from which Alban drank. Finally, as the sword fell on his neck, the second executioner lost his eyes, being unable to see the truth.

Alban was buried either in or near an established cemetery on the flower-covered hill where he fell, and began to attract a pilgrimage, with Germanus of Auxerre among the earlier visitors. Bede also maintains that a church was built above the grave, where many miracles occurred. The foundation of the abbey of St. Albans did not take place until 793, however, when Offa, King of Mercia, endowed a monastic church into which the relics of St. Alban were translated.

It seems likely that, by the ninth-century Danish invasions at least, the shrine was a popular draw, but the relics themselves became entangled in a number of ownership disputes, which the great thirteenth-century St. Albans chronicler, Matthew Paris, was

anxious to lay to rest. Matthew Paris was responsible for writing, and possibly illustrating, the lives of several Anglo-Saxon saints, **Wulfstan**, **Edward the Confessor**, and **Guthlac** among them. His *Life of St. Alban* is understandably the most closely argued, and relates how the relics of St. Alban were stolen by a Danish army in about 870 and removed to a monastery at Odense (Denmark), Alban himself permitting this theft because of the lax discipline of his own monastic community. Once the abbey of St. Albans had been reformed, he appeared in a vision to one of the monks, Egwin, telling him how he might retrieve the relics. Egwin travelled to Odense and presented himself at the monastery, asking to be received into the order. He rose to the position of sacrist, where it became his duty to guard the relics. One night, he bored a hole into the base of the reliquary casket, removed the relics, and gave them to a group of merchants for return to St. Albans. Claiming homesickness, Egwin then followed shortly afterwards.

In a second, fairly typical, tale of claim

ABOVE: *Life of St. Alban*. The abbey of St. Albans had the good fortune to number Matthew Paris, the great thirteenth-century chronicler and historian, among its monastic congregation. The Dublin manuscript illustrated here is thought by many scholars to be in his own hand. The illustrations were probably added by an assistant, although it is possible they were produced by Paris himself around 1230, comparatively early in his career. This tinted drawing shows the martrydom of St. Alban, while the executioner, blind to the truth, duly loses his eyes.

and counter-claim, two manuscripts describe the relics' removal to Ely for safe-keeping, shortly before the Norman Conquest. Relations between the abbeys became strained after St. Albans was informed that the bones Ely eventually returned to them were not those of Alban, but a worth-less skeleton. The St. Albans version augments this with their abbot's reply; that they had anticipated the trick, and sent only decoy relics in the first place. Recent archaeological attempts to locate the original burial place of St. Alban have proved unsuccessful.

Alphege *c.954-1012*
Martyr Feast day April 19

One of the leading figures in the tenth-century English monastic reform movement, Alphege had the most revered cult at Canterbury Cathedral prior to the murder of **Thomas Becket** in 1170. Virtually all that is known of Alphege is derived from five mentions in the *Anglo-Saxon Chronicle*, and Osbern's *Vita* of *c.*1090. From these we learn that Alphege was a monk at Deerhurst (Gloucestershire), and that after a period of solitude in Somerset, he was appointed Abbot of Bath by **Dunstan**, though the latter claim should be viewed with scepticism. Thenceforth his rise was rapid. In 984 he was created Bishop of Winchester in succession to **Aethelwold**, who had been a driving force behind the monastic reform movements. In 994 he acted as chief negotiator for Ethelred the Unready in a council with Swein Forkbeard, and in 1005 he was consecrated Archbishop of Canterbury.

In September, 1011, a Danish army laid siege to Canterbury, capturing the city after the archdeacon, Aelfmaer, went over to the opposition. Alphege and anyone else of note were imprisoned, and the Danes demanded ransoms, a particularly vast sum being placed on the head of the Archbishop. By the spring of 1012 the prisoners were held at Greenwich, and, though smaller ransoms had been paid for the nobility, Alphege forbade his people to pay any more, presumably in sympathy with Kipling's dictum "once you have paid the Danegeld/you will never get rid of the Dane." Incensed at the news, and having recently looted a wine-ship, a party of drunken Danes killed Alphege by pelting him with the bones of an ox recently consumed at a feast. The body was initially buried at St. Paul's Cathedral, London, but King Cnut was sufficiently anxious to encourage reconciliation between Anglo-Saxons and Danes that he allowed the body to be translated to Canterbury, and the Archbishop was reunited with his cathedral in 1023.

Ambrose *c.339-97*
Bishop and Doctor of the Church
Feast day December 7

Born into an old Gallo-Roman senatorial family in Trier, Ambrose rose quickly through the ranks of the Roman administrative system to be appointed provincial governor of Aemilia-Liguria in 370, whose seat was then at Milan. In common with the whole of late-fourth-century Mediterranean Europe, the church of Milan was embroiled in the dispute between Arian and Catholic Christians. On the death of the Arian bishop, Auxentius, in 374, Ambrose appealed for a peaceful election at the assembly called to decide a successor. Although he was undergoing training as a catechumen, Ambrose was not then a baptized Christian. He was therefore not unnaturally surprised at hearing his appeal interrupted by a voice crying "Ambrose for bishop." The cry was taken up by the assembly, Ambrose's objections were overruled, and he was simultaneously baptized, ordained and consecrated bishop on December 7, 374.

ABOVE: St. Alphege, in St. Mary's, Deerhurst.

RIGHT ABOVE: *The Four Doctors of the Church*, Jacob Jordaens. Bravura seventeeth-century altarpiece representing Ambrose, Gregory, Augustine and Jerome. Ambrose is to the left.

RIGHT BELOW: *St. Ambrose in his Study* (woodcut, printed in Basle, 1491). The scourge hanging from a bracket to the left of the saint's chair refers to the penance he imposed on Emperor Theodosius.

Auctor operum sequentium.

Scs Ambrosius Mediolanen
Eps: ecclesie doctor celeberrim?

The early years of Ambrose's episcopate were taken up with theological study under the Roman scholar Simplicianus, who encouraged him to read the Early Christian Greek writers, a study which influenced the treatise on the nature of faith he wrote for the emperor Gratian in 377. Gratian's sudden demise in 383 brought Ambrose into contact with Imperial politics at the highest level, and he was responsible for persuading the new western emperor, Maximus, not to move against the eastern emperor Valentinian II, famously informing the latter that "the emperor is in the Church, not above it."

The wisdom and clarity of Ambrose's sermons were particularly valued by **Augustine of Hippo**, and indeed were partly responsible for Augustine's conversion, and they were also widely read during the later Middle Ages. His most influential work was *De Officiis Ministrorum*, an ambitious treatment of Christian ethics, while his contribution to the liturgy is underscored by the few, extremely beautiful, Latin hymns to survive from his pen.

Ian. Luyken. invenit et fecit.

Andrew *First century*
Apostle and martyr
Feast day November 30

Identified as the brother of Simon Peter in all four gospels, Andrew was one of the fishermen of Bethsaida who were the first apostles of Christ. According to John, Andrew was a disciple of John the Baptist when he first encountered Christ, and was responsible for introducing Peter to "the Messiah." He is invariably among the first four names in the gospel lists of the apostles, but is not granted as intimate a role as that of the "inner circle" of Peter, James and John. He plays a significant part only in the Feeding of the Five Thousand and as a go-between for the Greeks who wished to meet Christ at the Feast of Passover.

The surviving accounts of Andrew's life after Pentecost are persistent, but unreliable. Eusebius of Caesarea, writing between 303 and 323, maintains that he preached in

ABOVE: *Martyrdom of St. Andrew*, engraving by Jan Luyken. Eighteenth-century image of Andrew crucified on a saltire cross outside the city gates of Patras.

LEFT: Images of the apostles beside the instruments of their martyrdom were commonplace from the early thirteenth century onward, though the landscape setting and theatrical piety of the painting shown here is very much a characteristic of the seventeenth and eighteenth centuries.

Scythia, while the early-third-century *Acts of St Andrew* alleges he was crucified at Patras in Achaia (Greece). Gregory of Tours repeats much of this account in his *Glory of the Martyrs* of *c.*590, and speaks of the tomb at Patras:

On the day of his festival the Apostle Andrew works a great miracle, that is manna with the appearance of flour, and oil with the fragrance of nectar, which overflows from his tomb. In this way the fertility of the coming year is revealed. If only a little oil flows, the land will produce few crops; but if the oil is plentiful it signifies that the fields will produce many crops. For they say that in some years so much oil gushed from his tomb that a torrent flowed into the middle of the church.

It is by no means easy to reconcile this account with the fourth-century belief that Andrew had founded the church of Constantinople, nor the story that Emperor Constantius sacked Patras in 345 and removed the body of Andrew to the Church of the Holy Apostles in Constantinople.

What is clear, however, is that relics of St. Andrew were highly prized during the early Middle Ages. Justinian's rebuilding of the Church of the Holy Apostles after 532 was believed to have enshrined the saint's relics, but innumerable accounts of portions of the saint traveling around Latin Europe suggest that either the body in Constantinople was not entire, or that another body, or bodies, had been claimed as Andrew. Gregory of Tours mentions some relics of Andrew in sixth-century Burgundy, and the church of San Pedro de la Rúa at Estella (Spanish Navarre) cherished his shoulder blade, while, most famously, St. Regulus brought a portion of the saint to Scotland. The latter journey is recorded in a mid-twelfth-century document, and though it is historically untenable in the form it takes there, it is clearly based on an actual journey and endowment. Modern scholarship considers this to have taken place during the early eighth century. The story goes that Regulus brought some relics of Andrew to Fife as a gift, where they were received by Hungus, who endowed a monastery at Kilrimont to enshrine them which subsequently became known as St. Andrews. The document speaks of him as having come from Patras, which is unlikely, but it is possible that Regulus was sent with them from Constantinople as a diplomatic gift, or that they were brought from Hexham for safe-keeping. With this established, Andrew was adopted as the patron saint of Scotland.

The tradition that Andrew was crucified on a saltire cross (X) cannot be dated any earlier than the tenth century, when it is mentioned in Autun. The symbol was adopted in Scotland, where it became known as St. Andrew's cross, and is the emblem of Scotland on the Union Jack. Representations of such crucifixions are even later still, and only became common during the late Middle Ages.

Anne *First century*
Mother of the Virgin Mary
Feast day July 26

Anne's name is first encountered in the mid-second-century *Protoevangelium of James*, where Anne and her husband Joachim are described as an elderly and childless couple, to whom an angel appears and announces that Anne will bear a child, whose name shall be Mary. Subject to medieval embellishment, this remains the basic legend of Anne. The cult seems to have become established in the East in the fourth century, and began to assume a

ABOVE: As may be seen from this mid-fourteenth century panel painting, the association of Andrew with the saltire cross did not gain widespread acceptance until well into the fifteenth century. The panel originally formed part of a large polyptych, and was probably painted in Siena *c.*1340.

firm date with which he can be associated is 651, when he entered the monastery of Melrose (Borders) as a novice. Eata, abbot of Melrose, had been a pupil of Aidan, the celebrated ex-Iona monk and founder of the monastery of Lindisfarne, and it seems likely that at this date Melrose was run on Celtic lines.

Promoted to the position of guest-master, Cuthbert traveled with Eata to establish a

LEFT: *St. Mark Enthroned between SS Cosmas, Damian, Roche, and Sebastian*, Titian, Venice, Sta Maria della Salute. This altarpiece was commissioned from Titian in late 1510 or 1511 and was intended as an offering in gratitude for the liberation of Venice from a great plague. It was to prove optimistic, for although the plague first struck in 1509 it continued throughout 1512 and recurred with diminishing intensity from 1513-15. It is presumably because it was painted at a time when there seemed little prospect of relief that St. Mark's head is in deep shadow. St. Mark is there as a personification of Venice, and the principal players are Cosmas and Damian (right), surgeons and healers, and Roch and Sebastian (left), intercessors against plague. The altarpiece was originally painted for the church of Santo Spirito in Isola, Venice.

uite & uirtucu et qlqs legerit inueniet.
'111 Quom adreligas qda mirifice fuerit ab octi languo
ſanati

monastery at Ripon on estates donated by Alhfrith, but after Alhfrith insisted on Roman usage, both were evicted in favor of Wilfrid. On their return in about 661, Cuthbert was made prior of Melrose. The question of Cuthbert's position during the disputes between the Roman and Celtic Churches over the calculation of the date of Easter is difficult. His earliest biographer maintains he was tonsured in the Roman manner (the familiar bald crown – the Celtic tonsure ran from ear to ear around the back of the skull), but he must have celebrated the Celtic Easter to have been displaced from Ripon by Wilfrid. This issue was referred to a Synod at Streoneshalh (usually identified as Whitby) in 663, where Colman, Bishop of Lindisfarne, presented the Celtic case and Wilfrid argued for Rome. Oswiu, King of Northumbria, came out in favor of Rome, with the result that Colman abandoned his see at Lindisfarne and returned to Iona. Presumably Eata and Cuthbert were among those Celtic-trained monks persuaded by the decision at Streoneshalh, for in 663 Eata was made abbot of the monks of Lindisfarne who had accepted the Roman reckoning, and soon afterward he asked Cuthbert to serve under him as prior.

Despite this acceptance of Roman authority, Cuthbert's life at Lindisfarne seems closer in spirit to Celtic eremitical monasticism than to the strict Benedictine Rule which Wilfrid was introducing at Ripon and Hexham. For a while, he retired to live as a hermit on St. Cuthbert's Isle, relatively close to the monastery, but in 676 he resigned his office of prior in order to withdraw into complete solitude on Inner Farne, an island some six miles south-east of Lindisfarne. It was here, among the birds and seals, that he enjoyed the reveries and contemplative union so eloquently described by Bede in his *Life of St. Cuthbert*. By 684 his reputation for holiness had become so great that Ecgfrith, King of Northumbria, came out to Inner Farne to plead with Cuthbert to accept the bishopric of Hexham. At first Cuthbert was reluctant, but he was eventually persuaded to trade bishoprics with Eata, then in charge of the diocese of Lindisfarne, and on March 26, 685, he was consecrated bishop, with Eata going to Hexham in Cuthbert's stead. The anonymous life written within a few years of Cuthbert's death speaks of him spending these last years traveling about the diocese, preaching, confirming the sheep farmers of the remote Northumbrian hills, and performing miracles. And on March 20, 687, having once more returned to Inner Farne, Cuthbert died.

The news of Cuthbert's death was signaled to the monks at Lindisfarne by lighted torches, and the following morning they carried their beloved bishop to Lindisfarne for burial near the monastic church. The habit of the early Middle Ages was to bury those regarded in their own lifetime as saints in an earth grave, so that the flesh might rot, and then to raise the body in order to wash the bones, wrap them in silks and place them in a shrine. This ceremony was known as "the elevation of the relics" and amounts to a declaration of sainthood. Eadbert, Bishop of Lindisfarne, allowed the elevation of Cuthbert's relics to take place on the eleventh anniversary of his death, in 698. When the body was raised, however, it was found to be incorrupt, a further sign of sainthood, and it was solemnly placed in a shrine on the sanctuary floor of the monastic church. The first miracles were reported within a year of Cuthbert's elevation, and by the time that Bede wrote his magisterial *De*

Vita et Miraculis Sancti Cuthberti in about 720, a considerable pilgrimage to the shrine had taken root.

The destination of this pilgrimage began to change after 875, when persistent Norse raids finally persuaded Bishop Eardulf to take the monks into exile, carrying the relics of St. Cuthbert with them. Their extraordinary odyssey took in Norham-on-Tweed, Ripon, Carlisle and Chester-le-Street, before Cuthbert found eventual peace at Durham in 995 and was enshrined in Bishop Aldhun's White Church. By this time, Cuthbert's shrine had acquired a number of sumptuous donations, given

LEFT: *The Lay of St. Cuthbert*. A diabolical feast is interrupted by St. Cuthbert, here dressed as a pilgrim, who wrestles with a devil over possession of a child.

during the stay at Chester-le-Street. King Athelstan donated an embroidered stole, maniple and girdle, along with a copy of Bede's *Life of St. Cuthbert*, to the community in about 934, while in 945 Edmund, King of Wessex, is recorded as having wrapped the body of St. Cuthbert in two Byzantine cloths "with his own hands."

The bishopric was translated along with the community, and after William Carilef was appointed Bishop of Durham, a second cathedral was begun. Cuthbert was translated to a new shrine behind the high altar in this cathedral on September 4, 1104; although its setting was altered by the construction of the chapel of the nine altars in the mid-thirteenth century, this was the position it occupied for the rest of the Middle Ages. Cuthbert's incorruption was once more verified at the translation, an achievement not to be dismissed in the face of a skeptical Anglo-Norman audience, and his status as the most popular saint of northern England is confirmed in innumerable medieval texts. Even Henry VIII's chantry commissioners were moved by the intactness of Cuthbert's body, and allowed it burial under the medieval shrine site. The body was last exhumed in 1828, when the fragmentary late-seventh-century wooden coffin, textiles, pectoral cross and portable altar were removed and lodged with the cathedral authorities. These are now displayed in Durham Cathedral treasury.

David *Sixth century*
Bishop and patron of Wales
Feast day March 1

Known in Welsh as Dewi or Dafydd, David was adopted as patron of Wales after his canonization by Pope Calixtus II in about 1120. An eighth-century Irish martyrology speaks of Bishop David of Menevia (modern St. David's), and gives March 1 as his feast. Beyond this the early medieval documents make little of David, and although the cult was certainly established in Pembrokeshire by the eighth century, the earliest surviving account of his life was only written *c.*1090 by Rhygyvarch, a son of the Bishop of St. David's. According to this, David was the son of a Cardigan chieftain, Sant, and was sent to study the Latin scriptures under one Paulinus the Scribe. After his ordination as a priest David founded twelve monasteries, including Crowland, Glastonbury and Menevia (St. David's), which were famous, according to Rhygy-

varch, for their severe discipline and saintly leadership. He then undertook a pilgrimage to Jerusalem, and took the leading role at the Synod of Brevi (Cardiganshire) *c.*560.

It is on this latter point, David's participation in the Synod of Brevi, that the hagiographer's principal aim becomes clear. Rhygyvarch maintains that David addressed the assembly with such eloquence that "he was made archbishop," and Menevia was thus endowed with metropolitan status. The whole objective of the life is to lend historical support to the claims of the Welsh bishops that they did not owe allegiance to Canterbury. The identification of David as first archbishop of Wales, along with his pilgrimage to Jerusalem, are pure fiction, though that does not mean that all Rhygyvarch's life is unreliable. A council was held at Brevi; David almost certainly did found Menevia; and the early rule seems to have been strict. The title *Aquaticus*, the Waterman, applied to David in a ninth-century document, would indicate that beer, mead or wine were not tolerated within the monastic precincts.

Denis *Died c.251*
Martyr Feast day October 9

According to a passage in Gregory of Tours' *Historiae*, written *c.*580, Denis was one of the seven "bishops" despatched to Gaul in the mid-third century. On reaching Paris his preaching converted many, and he established a Christian community on an island in the Seine. He fell foul of the Roman authorities, however, and after a short period of imprisonment, was taken to a hill and beheaded, along with his two companions, Eleutherius and Rusticus (the hill subsequently taking the title "Montmartre" or mount of the martyrs.) The bodies of all three martyrs were then fished out of the Seine and buried in the woods to the north of Paris.

A later life of St. Denis alleges that a Christian woman by the name of Catulla built a monument above the graves, which was replaced in about 465 by a basilica, and the complex archaeology of the site can be interpreted as revealing a fifth-century building. What is certain is that by the time Gregory of Tours was writing, a substantial church dedicated to St. Denis had taken shape, and that Aregunde, wife of Clothaire, King of the Franks, was buried there *c.*580. Gregory even alludes to the shrine arrangements in his *Glory of the Martyrs*:

FAR LEFT: St. Davids Cathedral seen from the east. Little is reliably known of the early history of the site of St. Davids, and the earliest portions of the present fabric date from *c.*1180. The complex and heterogeneous east end seen here consists of a late twelfth-century presbytery, late thirteenth-century south aisle and early fourteenth-century lady chapel, though all these areas were subsequently refurbished or extended between 1365 and 1523.

LEFT: St. Denis between two angels. Rheims cathedral; north portal of west front. The identification of the central figure as Denis is not without problems, but as he is shown in the robes of a priest and not with the pallium of an archbishop, he is more likely to be Denis than Nicasius, the other major Rheims cult of a martyr, who died through decapitation. The figure dates from *c.*1230-33 and originally would probably have carried his cranium in his hands. The angel to the left was at one time intended as Gabriel of the Annunciation, but the carrying of a censer indicates that when first carved the figure must have been conceived as the companion to a martyr.

Another man was not afraid to step on the holy tomb [of St. Denis], while he wished to strike with his spear at the gold dove [attached to the tomb]. Because there was a tower on top of the tomb, the man's feet slipped on each side. He crushed his testicles, stabbed himself in the side with his spear, and was found dead. Let no one doubt that this happened by chance, but by the judgment of God.

The church took a further step forward during the reign of Dagobert (628-39), who was lavish in his support for St. Denis, and who may have been responsible for introducing the first community of monks.

Another, very different, story begins to circulate in 830s, promoted by Hilduin, abbot of St-Denis between 814 and 840. In 827 Hilduin received a Greek manuscript of Dionysius the Areopagite's treatise *On the Celestial Hierarchies* from the Byzantine Emperor Michael II, and with the help of the monks produced a rough Latin translation in the monastic scriptorium. The issues are necessarily complicated, for the author of *On the Celestial Hierarchies* is not the Dionysius who appears in *Acts of the Apostles*, but a fifth-century Syrian monk whom modern scholars refer to as Pseudo-Dionysius. Nevertheless, Hilduin developed the theory that *his* St. Denis was all three figures – the early Christian martyr of Paris, Dionysius the Aeropagite who was converted by St. Paul in Athens, and the author of *On the Celestial Hierarchies*. Hilduin's identification was extremely clever, and a number of details of the life of Denis were rewritten to accommodate it, principally concerned with chronology. Thus after "Dionysius" was converted by Paul, he traveled to Rome and was commissioned by Pope Clement in about 90 AD to evangelize in Gaul. After his martyrdom in Paris, he was not rescued from the Seine but picked up his own head and walked with it to select his place of burial.

With this established, the new legend was broadly accepted, and under Abbot Suger (1122-51) a superb extension of the abbey was begun, which culminated in the consecration of the choir of the "Blessed Martyrs SS Denis, Eleutherius and Rusticus" on June 11, 1144. Suger also made a connection which was to have profound significance for later medieval France, for he established that Denis was lord of the Vexin, and that the King of France was therefore his vassal and should fight in his honor. Furthermore, the emblem of the Vexin was argued to be none other than the Oriflamme, Charlemagne's legendary battle standard, and as this was held in the abbey of St-Denis, French armies owed their allegiance to the saint. Denis had become the patron of France.

Domingo de la Calzada
1019-1109
Hermit Feast day May 12

Born in Viloria de Rioja (Spain), Domingo trained as a monk at the monastery of Valvanera. It seems unlikely that he ever took monastic vows, and in about 1050 he settled to the life of a hermit on the banks of the river Oja. Domingo de la Calzada translates as Dominic of the Causeway, and the title was bestowed after Domingo built a 24-arched bridge to carry the *Camino de Santiago*, the pilgrimage road to Santiago de Compostela in north-west Spain, across the river Oja. Aymery Picaud, writing in the 1130s, maintains he also "built the stretch of road between Nájera and Redecilla del Camino." Domingo subsequently constructed a pilgrim's hospice on the east bank of the river and founded a church on land donated by Alfonso VI of Castile *c.*1098. A significant town grew up alongside the bridge, known in the earlier documents as *Burgo de Santo Domingo*, and by 1232,

taking its title from the cathedral which developed above Domingo's earlier church, Santo Domingo de la Calzada.

Domingo is understandably celebrated as a patron and protector of pilgrims, and a number of late medieval miracles were attributed to his intercession. The most spectacular might be regarded as something of a type-miracle and occurs in several earlier legends, where it is considered the

$\mathfrak{S}$ IONISIVS

BELOW: St. Denis hands the oriflamme to Jean Clément, Maréchal de France (Chartres Cathedral). The glass was executed between 1228 and 1231, while Eudes, brother of Jean Clément, was abbot of St-Denis.

work of other saints. Nevertheless, by the late Middle Ages it is firmly attributed to Santo Domingo, and is frequently encountered in the memoirs of fifteenth- and sixteenth-century pilgrims. The form the story most commonly takes alleges that a family of French or German pilgrims were making their way to Santiago, and stopped for the night at an inn at Santo Domingo de la Calzada. The innkeeper's daughter took a fancy to the son, Hugonell, but her advances were spurned. Later that night she hid a silver goblet in Hugonell's scrip, and the following morning she took her revenge by denouncing him as a thief to the local *Corregidor* (magistrate). Hugonell was arrested, found guilty, and hanged, but as his parents were finally preparing to leave, they heard Hugonell whisper that he was alive on the gallows, his feet supported by Santo Domingo. They rushed to tell this to the Corregidor, as he was settling down to dine on a platter of roast cock and hen. The Corregidor retorted that Hugonell was no more alive than his dinner, at which the cock and hen leapt from the plate, sprouted feathers, and crowed the boy's innocence. A live cockerel and hen are still kept in a sixteenth-century coop in the cathedral of Santo Domingo de la Calzada in memory of the miracle.

Dominic *1170-1221*
Founder of the Dominican order
Feast day August 8

Dominic was born at Calaruega (Castile) into an old Castilian family named Guzman, and educated at Palencia. He was appointed a canon of the Augustinian community which served the cathedral of Osma in 1199, rising to the position of prior some two years later. Selected by Diego, Bishop of Osma, to be his companion in preaching against the Cathars (or Albigensians) in Languedoc in either 1203 or 1204, Dominic initially settled in Toulouse, before deciding to work in those rural areas where Catharism had its strongest following. Accordingly he moved to Prouille, where he founded a nunnery in 1206, intending to encourage the formation of a strict Catholic life whose ascetic rigor might compare favorably with that of the Cathar *parfaits*. The murder of the papal legate, Pierre de Castelnau, in 1208 put an end to such subtle methods, and Pope Innocent III's decision to declare an Albigensian Crusade, a vicious campaign which lasted from 1208-18, made

life difficult for those, like Dominic, who saw patient persuasion, rather than mass extermination, as the way to deal with Catharism.

Dominic's great achievement was the foundation of the *Ordo Praedicatorum*, or Friars Preachers (in France also known as Jacobins and in England as Black Friars). This had its origins at Casseneuil, a castle Simon de Montfort made over to Dominic in 1214, where the initial ideas for an order devoted to winning Cathars back to the Church were first developed. Dominic attracted a number of followers, and the community was formally recognized as a religious house by the Bishop of Toulouse in 1215. The decrees of the Fourth Lateran Council of the same year stipulated that new orders should take on an existing Rule, and when Honorius III finally in 1216 issued papal decrees recognizing the community as an order, Dominic was forced to take the Augustinian Rule as his basis. Nonetheless new members were quick to join, and by

FAR LEFT: *St. Dominic* by Fra Angelico. The figure is a detail from a *Mocking of Christ*, painted some time between 1438 and 1446 on the walls of Cell 7 in the reformed Dominican convent of San Marco, Florence.

ABOVE: St. Dominic supervises the burning of heretical texts by the fifteenth-century Castilian artist Pedro Berruguete.

1219 a number of Dominican friaries had been established in Italy, France and Spain.

The first General Chapter was held in Bologna in 1220, and approved the constitution which informed the character of the Dominican order for the whole of the Middle Ages; a body of intellectual priests who might live on a communal basis, but who were principally concerned with work in the community, with teaching, preaching, and bringing the heretical back into the Church. The argumentative rigor of Dominicans became legendary, attracting intellectuals of the caliber of Albertus Magnus and Thomas Aquinas. While their late medieval identification as *Domini Canes*, hounds of God, is unfair when applied to the thirteenth century, it was wholly apposite in the fourteenth, when the order provided the Church with most of the staff for its Inquisition. The great houses were also frequently sited in university cities; it was no coincidence that three of the greatest houses founded in Dominic's lifetime were in Paris, Bologna and Oxford. Dominic himself died in Bologna in 1221, was canonized in 1234, and enshrined in a magnificent tomb commissioned from Nicola Pisano and Arnolfo di Cambio in 1264.

Dunstan *c.910-88*
Monk and archbishop Feast day May 19

ABOVE: St. Dunstan, shown in a nineteenth-century engraving. The demon featured top right is here seen escaping from Dunstan's crozier.

Born at Baltonsborough (Somerset) and educated at Glastonbury, Dunstan was related to the royal house of Wessex, and after spending some time at the court of his uncle, Athelm, then Archbishop of Canterbury, he was recruited to serve King Athelstan in Wessex. It seems that Dunstan was unpopular with the other nobles in the king's household, and after contemplating marriage he was persuaded by Aelfheah, Bishop of Winchester, to make his profession as a monk. Aelfheah subsequently ordained Dunstan priest, on the same day as his great friend and contemporary, **Aethelwold**. With the accession of Edmund as king of Wessex in 939, Dunstan was once more brought into government, and some time before the winter of 940 was installed as abbot of Glastonbury. He spent the next 15 years here, launching a program of new building works in 944, and reforming the monastic chapter along strict Benedictine lines.

The major turning-point in Dunstan's life was his banishment by King Eadwy in 955. This seems to have been caused by some personal slight, and Dunstan chose to spend his exile at the monastery of St. Peter's, Ghent (Belgium), one of the great centers of the European monastic reform movement. Here Dunstan was exposed to monastic thinking on the Continent, and the experience had a profound influence on the subsequent development of the Anglo-Saxon reform movement. Dunstan was recalled by Edgar of Wessex in 957 and invited to take up the bishopric of Worcester, an appointment which was rapidly followed by his promotion to London in 959, and finally to his consecration as Archbishop of Canterbury in 960. In 961 Dunstan also persuaded King Edgar to invite Oswald, who had been trained at the great French abbey of Fleury (St.-Benoît-sur-Loire), to become Bishop of Worcester and Archbishop of York. With Aethelwold created Bishop of Winchester in 963, the scene was set for the monastic reform to begin in earnest.

These three men, with the active encouragement of King Edgar, all of whose lives were so closely interwoven, transformed English religious life during the second half of the tenth century. Dunstan was the catalyst, and after the mid-970s he increasingly took a background role. Nevertheless it was his initial reform of Glastonbury which sparked the revival, and his courting of Oswald, Aethelwold and the Continental monks which gave it critical mass. Dunstan was personally responsible for the foundation or refoundation of the abbeys of Athelney, Malmesbury, Bath, Muchelney and Westminster, and the rededication of the old abbey of SS Peter and Paul at Canterbury to St. Augustine. Like Aethelwold he was also a practicing artist, skilled in painting, embroidery and metalwork, and he attached great importance to the role of the artist-monk.

Dunstan's last years were spent almost exclusively among the monks at Christchurch, Canterbury, preoccupied with teaching and supervising the scriptorium. His death, on May 19, 988, occasioned much mourning and his body was buried "in the midst of the choir" in Canterbury Cathedral, the cause, in later years, of a celebrated quarrel with Glastonbury over rights to the possession of Dunstan's relics. Following the completion of the early twelfth-century choir at Canterbury Cathedral, Dunstan's relics were translated. Most unusually, the Romanesque shrine arrangements were described by a monk at Canterbury, Gervase, whose recollection was prompted by the destruction of the choir in 1174. Dunstan was given an altar to contain his relics just to the south of the high altar, and opposite that of St. **Alphege**.

At the eastern horns of the [high] altar were two wooden columns, gracefully ornamented with gold and silver, and sustaining a great beam, the extremities of which rested upon the capitals of two of the pillars [of the main arcade]. This beam, carried across the church above the altar, and decorated with gold, sustained the representations of the Lord, and the images of St. Dunstan and St. Alphege, together with seven chests filled with the relics of divers saints.

Edmund *c.841-69*
King and martyr Feast day November 20

Raised the Christian son of a king of "Saxony", Edmund was chosen as king of the East Angles some time before 865. The principal account of Edmund's martyrdom, the *Passio Sancti Edmundi*, was written at Ramsey Abbey, probably between 985 and 987, by Abbo of Fleury, who maintains he is

LEFT: Most popular representations of St. Dunstan show him as a bishop holding a demon by the nose with a pair of tongs.

transcribing a tale Edmund's standard-bearer related to St. **Dunstan** (909-88). This is just plausible, but whatever its merits, Abbo was certainly recording an established oral tradition. According to Abbo, Edmund was captured after being defeated in battle by the Norse army of Ingwar in 869. Ingwar bartered his life in exchange for a

BELOW: Miniature of *c.*1170, painted in the scriptorium of Christchurch, Canterbury, and depicting Dunstan amending the Benedictine Rule, from the *Commentary on the Rule of St. Benedict.*

half share of the kingdom, but Edmund refused to co-operate with a pagan. He was taken to Hellesdon (Norfolk), tied to a tree, and shot full of arrows until he resembled "a thistle." His head was then removed, and was said to have been guarded by a wolf until it could be recovered. He was initially buried nearby, but in about 915 the body was found to be incorrupt and was moved to Bedricsworth (subsequently known as Bury St. Edmunds).

Abbo's narrative does not extend much further than this, but by the late ninth century a considerable cult of St. Edmund had developed, witnessed, for instance, by the minting of coins bearing the legend *Sc. Eadmund Rex*. King Athelstan founded a community of priests to care for Edmund in 925, and some time before 950 his body was shown to Theodore, Bishop of London. The cult received a further boost in the eleventh century, when Cnut replaced the secular priests with monks, and **Edward the Confessor** added most of west Suffolk to the earlier donations of land. These enormous estates formed the basis of the abbey of Bury St. Edmunds' wealth and prestige during the Middle Ages. The actual display of Edmund's relics took a curious turn, however. Between 1044 and 1065 Edmund's

ABOVE: St. Edmund martyred by the Danes, fifteenth-century wall painting from SS Peter and Paul, Pickering, Yorkshire, showing Edmund on a characteristically late medieval floral background.

RIGHT: Edward the Confessor, detail from the left panel of the *Wilton Diptych* c.1395/99.

coffin was once more opened and his incorruptibility confirmed, but the head was firmly attached to the body, and even a tug-of-war between the abbot and the monks could not separate the two. It was declared that they had been miraculously reunited. There were subsequent openings of the coffin in 1095, when Abbot Baldwin translated Edmund to a new choir, and after a fire in 1198, when Jocelyn of Brakelond remarked that the body seemed too big for its earlier setting, and a new shrine was inaugurated. The latter seems to have been a very grand and unusual affair, with the shrine set high above the ritual choir, and the body said to be visible. Royal saints always attract a political following and Edmund was no exception, being seen in the later Middle Ages as a royal patron of England.

Edward the Confessor
c.1004-66
King Feast day October 13

Edward was the son of the Anglo-Saxon King Ethelred II (the Unready), and his second wife, Emma of Normandy. Following Cnut's accession as sole ruler of England in 1016, Edward was sent with his brother, Alfred, to be educated in the ducal court at Rouen, and only returned to England at the invitation of Cnut's son, Harthacnut, in 1041. Harthacnut nominated Edward his successor, and on his death in 1042 Edward was acclaimed king in London, and crowned in Winchester Cathedral on Easter Sunday, 1043. Historians are divided in their assessments of Edward's reign. Some characterize Edward as an insubstantial figure, fatally weakened in his dealings with Danish and Norman pretenders to the English throne by poor judgment. Others stress his ability to maintain peace in a country which was riven by factional interests, keeping the lid on quarrels between the Anglo-Saxon nobility under Godwine of Wessex, the Danes under Beorn and Swein Estrithson, and Edward's own Norman appointees at court. Edward was certainly forced to make compromises, acquiescing in the deposition of the Norman Robert Champart as Archbishop of Canterbury, after London was disturbed by anti-Norman riots in 1051. Although he did make mistakes, however, his reign was crucial in re-opening commercial and intellectual links with Continental Europe.

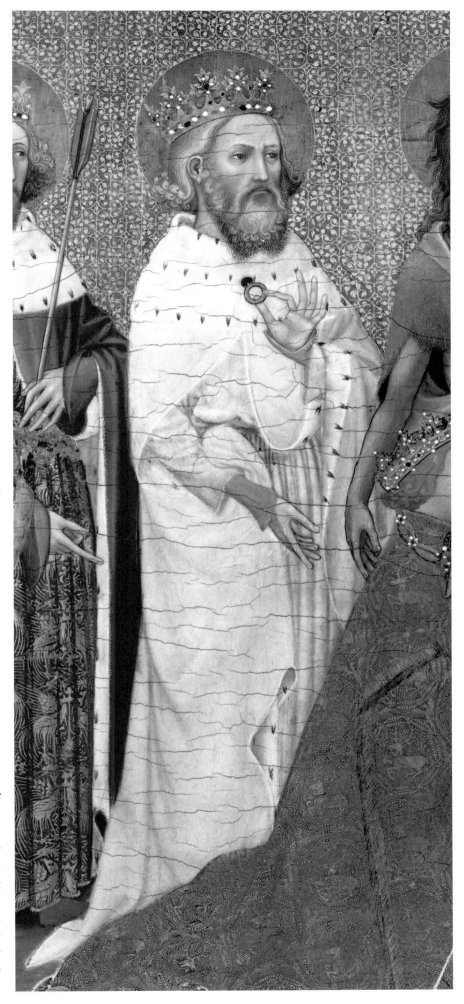

Edward's reputation for piety is well documented, and turns on his charity to the poor, celibacy (it was believed his marriage to Edith was unconsummated), and personal devotion. He supported Leo IX's call at the 1049 Council of Rheims for the elimination of simony and nepotism in the Church, and around 1050 effectively relaunched Westminster Abbey as a major Benedictine monastery. Edward took a close personal interest in the rebuilding of Westminster, and must have been respon-

sible for the decision to model the church on the abbey of Notre-Dame de Jumièges. As such, Westminster was the first major building in England which might be described as Romanesque. It was also intended to act as his place of burial, and Edward rushed through the consecration of the choir on December 28, 1065, in readiness to receive his body after his death on January 5, 1066.

An anonymous life of Edward, written between 1065 and 1067, attributes several

ABOVE: *Edward and the Pilgrim* (Forthampton Court, Gloucestershire), panel painting of *c.*1370 depicting Edward the Confessor handing a ring to a pilgrim. Similar figures in silver originally stood to either side of the Confessor's thirteenth-century shrine at Westminster.

miracles to him, and maintains he could cure scrofula (known in the Middle Ages as the King's Evil) by the touch of his hand. Nonetheless the cult was slow in taking off, and the motivation behind attempts to have him canonized was wholly political. King Stephen was the first to petition the papacy, in 1138, but Innocent II was unconvinced and demanded that the monks at Westminster collate more information in Edward's support. Henry II (Plantagenet) tried again in 1160, and traded his support for Pope Alexander III against the antipope Victor IV, in return for canonization. This was approved in 1161, and on October 13, 1163, the relics of St. Edward were solemnly translated into a shrine at Westminster Abbey. A second life of Edward was written by the great Cistercian scholar, Ailred of Rievaulx, and as a definite "top-person's saint" the cult began to grow.

Any wider popularity enjoyed by Edward is due to Henry III (1216-72). It was Henry who, "moved by the devotion he had for St. Edward, ordered the church of St. Peter at Westminster to be enlarged" (Matthew Paris: *Chronica Majora*). Matthew Paris' entry is under the year 1245, and it announces the rebuilding of Westminster Abbey, which culminated in a magnificent translation of the relics of St. Edward to a new shrine behind the high altar on October 13, 1267. Henry even commissioned a new version of Ailred of Rievaulx's life from Matthew Paris, and in this form the *Vita Edwardi* was much quoted. The story of Edward and the pilgrim also became popular, and features in a number of surviving paintings, stained glass windows and ceramic tiles. This tells that Edward was importuned by a beggar, in fact St. **John the Evangelist** in disguise, to whom he gave a ring. Some time later St. John revealed himself to two English pilgrims in the Holy Land (said to be from Ludlow in some versions) and handed them the ring, instructing them to restore it to the king on their return, and inform him that within six months they would meet in Paradise. This the pilgrims did, and shortly afterward Edward died.

Elizabeth of Hungary
1207-31
Princess Feast day November 17

Daughter of Andrew II, King of Hungary, Elizabeth was married in 1221 to the Landgrave of Thuringia, Ludwig IV, by whom she

had three children. By all accounts it was an extremely happy marriage, and what was a political match seems to have blossomed into an intense and passionate relationship, mostly spent in the castle at Wartburg. Ludwig's death at Ótranto (Apulia) in 1227, while joining Frederick II's intended Crusade, extinguished this, and it was said that when the news reached Elizabeth her screams filled the castle for days. She left Wartburg that winter, driven out by her brother-in-law, Henry Raspe; the more heart-rending accounts have her thrown into the snow with a baby at her breast.

In 1228 Elizabeth accepted the direction of her confessor, Conrad of Marburg, and took a house at Marburg (Hesse). The few remaining years of her life were spent here working as a Franciscan tertiary, sewing garments for the poor and ministering to the sick in a hospital she constructed close to her home. Her death was certainly hastened by the sadistic treatment she received at the

ABOVE: *St. Elizabeth of Hungary Nursing the Sick* by the seventeenth-century Spanish artist Bartolomé Estebán Murillo. Elizabeth seen in the hospital she founded toward the end of her life in Marburg.

SCA CLARA   SCISABETTA

hands of Conrad, who dismissed the household she brought with her from Wartburg, and whose suggested penitential acts included much physical violence. Elizabeth turned down all secular advice to remarry, as well as the invitation of her family to return to Hungary, dying at the age of 24 in 1231. She was canonized in 1235, the same year that the Elisabethskirche at Marburg was begun to enshrine her remains.

Etheldreda *c.630-79*
Virgin and abbess Feast day June 23.
Feast of the translation of relics October 17

Daughter of Anna, king of East Anglia, and traditionally thought to have been born at Exning (Suffolk), Etheldreda was married to Tondberht in about 652 and presented with the Isle of Ely as a dowry, but the marriage remained unconsummated and on Tondberht's death she retired to Ely. A second marriage was forced on her in 660, to Ecgfrith, son of Oswiu, King of Northumbria, but Etheldreda's agreement was conditional on Ecgfrith allowing her to remain a virgin. Ecgfrith's demand, in 672, that he be given full conjugal rights precipitated a bitter dispute, and advised by Wilfrid, then Archbishop of York, Etheldreda abandoned him and took the veil at Coldingham (Lothian). Ecgfrith remarried, and in 673 Etheldreda journeyed south and founded a double monastery at Ely.

Etheldreda spent the last seven years of her life at Ely, organizing the liturgical observances in what rapidly became the pre-eminent monastic community in East Anglia. Like virtually all early Anglo-Saxon foundations, this community was decidedly aristocratic, and Etheldreda was swiftly joined by other members of her family, among them her sister, Sexburga, and great-niece, Walburgh. Her own life at Ely was built around acts of personal renunciation, wearing hair or woollen garments and taking only one meal a day, and her emphasis on the importance of prayer was taken as a model for the whole community. As with Cluny in its early days, the atmosphere seems to have been that of a closely-knit and intimate family. Etheldreda's death in 679 was preceded by the appearance of a tumor on her neck, which a doctor tried and failed to remove, and she was buried in an earth grave in the monastic precincts. When the body was raised some 16 years later, the tumor was found to have healed and her relics to be incorrupt. She was laid in an old

Roman sarcophagus and formally translated to a new resting place by Sexburga on October 17, 695. This became the focus of one of the most important pilgrimages of early medieval England.

Eustace *Second century?*
Martyr Feast day September 20

The earliest accounts of Eustace's life are seventh century, and maintain that Eustace was martyred, along with his wife and two sons, under Emperor Hadrian in about 118. He had been converted to Christianity while hunting in the forests of Guadagnolo (near Palestrina, Lazio), where he experienced a vision of a stag with a crucifix caught in its antlers. This vision was subsequently added to the legend of St. Hubert, and although its origins are obscure, it has points in common with several ancient tribal myths from central Asia. Modern scholars believe that this, and other stories

FAR LEFT: *St. Elizabeth of Hungary and St. Clare*, Simone Martini (Assisi, lower church of San Francesco). The arrangement of saints at dado level in the chapel of St. Martin is a roll-call of those favored within the Franciscan order. Elizabeth (right) is here paired with Clare.

ABOVE: St. Etheldreda, from the *Benedictional of St. Aethelwold*. Aethelwold reformed the monastery of Ely during the 970s, and an indication of the esteem in which he held its church and relics is his inclusion of Etheldreda in the *Benedictional* of 971-84.

An attempt in 1428 to convince the French commander at Vaucouleurs of the authenticity and usefulness of her voices failed, but Joan won considerable local support, and in February 1429, in the company of six soldiers, set out from Domrémy to seek an audience with the heir to the French throne, the Dauphin, at Chinon. She arrived on March 6 and lodged in town while waiting for an audience at the château. When one was granted two days later the Dauphin, the future Charles VII, attempted to disguise himself by swapping robes with a courtier. Undeceived by this ruse, Joan addressed Charles directly, saying "The King of Heaven sends words by me that you shall be annointed and crowned in the city of Reims. You are the heir to France and true son of the king." Given that his father was mad and his mother had taken a number of lovers, Charles was notoriously plagued by doubts as to his own legitimacy, but he seems to have been wholly convinced by Joan and, after her case had been examined by a theological court at Poitiers, gave her command of an army. On April 26 she raised her standard at Blois; on May 8 she relieved Orléans; and, having inflicted two serious defeats on the English in June, finally persuaded Charles to accompany her to Reims, where his coronation was celebrated on July 17.

This should have completed her mission, indeed her voices cautioned she did not have long to live, but it seems likely that she became intoxicated by her military successes. A failed autumn attack on Paris was followed by a stand-off, but Joan resumed campaigning in the spring of 1430. It was to prove her undoing. Having relieved Compiègne of occupation by the Burgundian allies of the English, she was captured on May 24 when leading a small party of troops out from one of the city gates. The question of what to do with her remained unresolved for some time, but finally, on November 21, through the mediation of Pierre Cauchon, Bishop of Beauvais, Joan was ransomed for 10,000 ducats and handed over to the English captain of Rouen, Richard of Warwick. She was imprisoned in a tower of Philip Augustus's old castle to the north of the cathedral in Rouen, while Warwick reinforced the city against the possibility of popular uprising. On February 21, 1431, Bishop Cauchon opened the first session of her trial on charges of witchcraft and heresy. The trial lasted three months, and after further examination in her cell, a sum-mary of her statements was compiled. Her visions were pronounced "false and diabolical," and she was found "heretical and schismatic" and led to the scaffold in the cemetery of St-Ouen. The precise nature of events here is a matter of controversy. Encouraged by a large crowd to recant, Joan did make some sort of repudiation of her former testimony. What form this took is uncertain, but it was enough to convince the English to commute her sentence to one of life imprisonment. Cauchon's determination was not to be brooked, however, and on Trinity Sunday her English captors tricked her into wearing a man's clothes in the prison courtyard, thus breaking a vow it was said she made on recanting her crimes. On May 30 she was led to the Place du Vieux-Marché and burned at the stake as a witch, the terrified English guards throwing her unconsumed heart into the river Seine. The zeal with which her captors pursued her death is a measure of the influence she exercised, and the whispered misgivings of the English soldiery eroded their already tenuous belief in an English future in northern France. In 1449 Charles VII entered Rouen unopposed and, with the help of the Franciscan Hélie de Bourdeilles, set in motion the procedures which led to Pope Callixtus III declaring Joan innocent in 1456. She was formally canonized by Pope Benedict XV in 1920, and recognized as the second patron of France, after the great medieval protector of France, St. Denis.

Joan is usually depicted fully armed and the sources attest to her wearing a suit of white armor. The 1431 trial deposition records that she refused the sword Charles offered her at Chinon, and instead despatched soldiers to fetch her a sword from the pilgrimage chapel of Ste-Catherine-de-Fierbois (Indre-et-Loire): "The best is found behind the altar of Ste-Catherine which I much love. You will find it easily, it is marked with five crosses." The chapel of Ste-Catherine was believed to have been founded by Charles Martel, the grandfather of Charlemagne; it was thought he left his sword there in thanksgiving after his great victory over the Moors in 732. By about 1380 a tradition had grown up that knights returning from battle would also offer a sword to the chapel. It was almost certainly one of these, a late-fourteenth-century sword, that Joan wielded, but from this grew the legend that Joan fought with the sword of Charles Martel, a powerful connection to make in late medieval France.

FAR LEFT: Gilded statue of Joan of Arc (Paris, nineteenth-century). Joan is seen fully armed, and carrying the standard she first raised at Blois on April 26, 1429.

John the Apostle
First century
Apostle Feast day December 27

John is traditionally thought to be the author of the Fourth Gospel, the *Book of Revelation* and three New Testament *Epistles*. The so-called synoptic gospels (those bearing the names of Matthew, Mark and Luke) identify John as one of the sons of Zebedee and the brother of James, who worked as a fisherman on the Sea of Tiberias before being called to become an apostle of Christ. He belonged to that small "inner group" of disciples who witnessed the Raising of Jairus' Daughter, the Transfiguration of Christ, and the Agony in the Garden. Like his brother James, he was evidently passionate and quick-tempered, and on a number of occasions Christ refers to them both as "Boanerges" (sons of thunder). After the Ascension, John developed a close relationship with Peter, and *Acts of the Apostles* frequently mentions the two together. They shared imprisonment in Jerusalem, conducting a joint defence before the Sanhedrin, and were asked by the other apostles to work together in bringing the Holy Spirit to the new converts of Samaria.

The fourth gospel never mentions John by name, nor indeed does it identify its author, but the Prologue can be interpreted as meaning the writer was a witness to the events he describes. The identification of this author as John is extremely early, and the view is shared by such noted late second-century writers as Clement of Alexandria and Irenaeus, and the discovery of an early fragment of chapter 18, the *Rylands St. John Papyrus* (John Rylands Library, Manchester), suggests the gospel was written before 120 AD. The view that it was written by John the Apostle rests on the assumption that the witness referred to as "the disciple whom Jesus loved" was John. This disciple certainly appears where one might expect to find John but, as so many of the events narrated in the synoptic gospels are absent, the evidence is far from conclusive. Nevertheless, "the disciple whom Jesus loved" was present at the Last Supper, where he lay on the breast of Christ; stood at the foot of the Cross and was entrusted with the care of the Virgin Mary; and was the first to recognize the Resurrected Christ at the Sea of Tiberias.

The sophisticated exegesis, spirituality,

and discursive style of the fourth gospel is quite different from the narrative concerns of the three other gospels (Matthew, Mark and Luke), and a number of theologians have argued that it presupposes, on the part of the reader, a knowledge of the principal events of the life of Christ as related in the synoptic gospels. It is largely because of its wrestling with philosophical questions of Faith, Resurrection, and Eternal Life, that its impact on later Christian thought was so profound. And although modern scholarship is inclined to see it as having been written by a disciple of John, rather than John himself, relatively few dismiss the case for the fourth gospel as a direct reflection of his teaching. That teaching is likely to have been conducted in Ephesus, for the tradition that John settled at Ephesus in Asia Minor (modern Turkey), was exiled to the island of Patmos by the Emperor Domitian in the early 90 AD, and returned to Ephesus, where he died c.100 AD, is again very early.

ABOVE: St John seen as author of the Fourth Gospel; prefatory Evangelist portrait from a Carolingian gospel book.

RIGHT ABOVE: *The Assumption of John the Evangelist* (Giotto: Peruzzi chapel, Sta Croce, Florence). Giotto's rendering of an unusual scene probably dates from c.1325.

RIGHT BELOW: Deposition group, San Joan de les Abadesses. This striking group of painted wooden figures was installed in the Catalan church of San Joan in 1251. John stands between the bad thief and Nicodemus.

John the Baptist
Died c.30 AD
Forerunner of Jesus Christ Feast days
June 24 (nativity) and August 29
(decollation)

John was the son of Zacharias, a priest at the Temple of Jerusalem, and Elizabeth, a cousin of the Virgin Mary. The couple were childless and Elizabeth was past child-bearing age. The story of John's birth is recounted by Luke, who speaks of the visit of the angel Gabriel to Zacharias: "Fear not, Zacharias; for thy prayer is heard; and thy wife Elizabeth shall bear thee a son, and thou shalt call his name John."

It seems likely that John was in his mid-20s when he began preaching in Judaea, a ministry which is reported in similar terms in all four gospels. Mark describes it as "The voice of one crying in the wilderness, Prepare ye the way of the Lord, make his paths straight. John did baptize in the wilderness, and preach the baptism of re-pentance for the remission of sins." John's way of life was based on that of the more ascetic Old Testament prophets, clothed in "camel's hair" and eating locusts and wild honey, but his teaching was of the imminence of the Messiah: "I indeed baptize you with water; but one mightier than I cometh, the latchet of whose shoes I am unworthy to unloose: He shall baptize you with the Holy Ghost."

An immensely charismatic figure, John attracted a number of followers, the future apostle Andrew among them, all of whom he baptized in the river Jordan. According to John's gospel, it was while he was at Beth-abara that John met Jesus. He greeted him with the words, "Behold the Lamb of God, which taketh away the sin of the world," and then baptized him. Shortly afterward he was imprisoned, for denouncing the incestuous union between Herod Antipas and Herodias, and although he was able to communicate with Christ from prison, as recorded by Luke, Matthew reports his death before the narrative of the Feeding of

BELOW: *The Beheading of John the Baptist* by Pierre Puvis de Chavannes, the foremost French mural painter of the later nineteenth century.

RIGHT: *The Baptism of Christ*, Piero della Francesca. Piero situates the Baptism in a valley close to his home town of Borgo San Sepolcro, on the borders of Tuscany and Umbria. The man pulling off his shirt in the background, his head covered, serves as a reminder that baptism is a casting off of the old Adam and an embracing the new. The painting is undated, but perhaps belongs to the 1450s.

the Five Thousand. The gospels lay the blame for his execution squarely on Herodias. After Salome, the daughter of Herodias, had pleased Herod with her dancing at his birthday feast, Herod promised her whatever she wished "unto the half of my kingdom." "And she went forth, and said unto her mother, What shall I ask? And [Herodias] said, The head of John the Baptist" (Mark $6^{23\text{-}24}$). Not without regret, Herod sent an executioner to deal with John in prison, and the severed head was brought to Salome on a platter. Thus, as Augustine writes, an oath rashly made was criminally kept.

The *Antiquities* of Josephus identifies the place of John's death as the fort of Machaerus on the Dead Sea, but an early tradition asserts he was buried at Sebaste (Samaria), where his tomb was despoiled by Emperor Julian the Apostate in about 362. Thereafter his relics seem to have been dispersed, and during the Middle Ages the best part of a dozen churches claimed possession of his head. His cult is both early and significant, however, and two of the Fathers of the Church, **Augustine of Hippo** and **Jerome**,

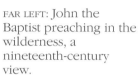

lay great stress on the celebration of the feast of his nativity. John's role as the herald of Christ and his institution of the sacrament of baptism were of fundamental importance for the development of the Church.

FAR LEFT: John the Baptist preaching in the wilderness, a nineteenth-century view.

ABOVE LEFT: The Baptism of Christ engraved on a Carolingian rock crystal. Engraved rock crystals were an extremely popular, if expensive, vehicle for narrative imagery at the Carolingian court. The Rouen crystal is unusual in featuring the Baptism of Christ, and was probably engraved in Metz *c*.860. The inclusion of an angel holding a cloth derived from early Christian sources.

LEFT : The Baptism of Christ, Arian Baptistry, Ravenna. This mosaic is at the center of the dome of the Arian bapristry (now known as Sta Maria in Cosmedin), and was probably designed in the reign of Theodoric the Ostrogoth *c*.495 AD. Christ is represented as a decidedly boyish figure, while John the Baptist wears a cloak of camel's hair, and the personification of the river Jordan is bizarrely embellished with a pair of lobster-claws on his head.

John Chrysostom
347-407
Patriarch Feast day September 13 (West),
November 13 (East)

Born to an army family in Antioch, John was educated in law by the noted pagan orator Libanius, and in Christian theology by Diodore of Tarsus. Between *c.*373 and 381 he lived as a hermit in the mountains above Antioch, but returned to the city as his health began to fail, where he served as a deacon. After his ordination as priest in 386, Bishop Flavian took him on as an assistant, giving him the responsibility of instructing the poor in the Scriptures. His sermons earned him the epithet *chrysostom* (golden-mouthed), and during the late 380s and 390s he wrote the *Homilies* on *Genesis, John* and, above all, the *Epistles*, for which he is best remembered. The importance of the *Homilies* lies with their clear exposition of spiritual truth and practical meaning, and like other theologians of the "Antioch School," John denied the validity of the allegorical interpretation of Scripture.

His reputation as a strong opponent of imperial corruption led Emperor Arcadius to obtain John's election as Patriarch of Constantinople in 398, an appointment which caused his death. His attempts at a moral reform of both the clergy and the court invited the hostility of Empress Eudoxia, while Theophilus, Patriarch of Alexandria, exploited the situation to avenge his disappointment at not having gained the see of Constantinople himself. In July, 403, at Chalcedon, Theophilus packed a synod with aggrieved Syrian and Egyptian bishops, and had John condemned on 29 counts, including the charge of treason for having described Eudoxia as "Jezebel." The accusations were trumped-up, but John was briefly sent into exile, before an earthquake seems to have worried the court into recalling him to Constantinople. John's resumption of the attack on lax morality, prostitution and favoritism at court, and on Jewish traders in the city, prompted Eudoxia and Theophilus to have him thrown out once more on a trumped-up charge. His banishment to Cucusus in Armenia was opposed by the Western Church, but the petitions proved fruitless and John eventually died on the road to the southern Black Sea coast, exhausted by a deliberate regime of forced bad-weather marches on foot.

John of the Cross *1542-91*
Carmelite friar and mystic
Feast day December 14

Born Juan de Yepes, he joined the Carmelites at Medina del Campo (Castile) in 1563, before being sent to study theology at Salamanca, where he was ordained a priest in 1567. Dissuaded by Theresa of Ávila from joining the Carthusian order, John adopted Theresa's Carmelite reform and attached himself to the first of the new *discalced* (barefoot) houses for men at Duruelo. In 1572 he became confessor to the Carmelite nuns at Ávila, but was arrested following the

ABOVE: St. John of the Cross, Carmelite convent of San Juan de la Cruz, Sanlúcar la Mayor, Andalucia. Detail of an eighteenth-century retable showing John of the Cross inspired by the Holy Spirit.

1575 Carmelite General Chapter at Piacenza and imprisoned in Toledo, the Chapter having refused to recognize the Discalced reform. He escaped from prison within a year and made his way south, founding a college at Baeza (Andalusia) in 1579, and subsequently acting as prior at Granada and Segovia. The Discalced Carmelites were in fact recognized in 1580, but John came to disagree with the policies of Nicolás Doria, Reformist Vicar General, and toward the end of his life was banished to Úbeda (Andalusia), where he died in 1591.

These few spare details of John's movements formed the background to the writing of some of the most moving religious and mystical poetry ever to emerge from Europe, much of it written in conditions of appalling hardship. A small man, who seems to have captivated most who met him with his generosity and warm-heartedness, John fell foul of the ecclesiastical politics of sixteenth-century Spain. Yet the poems he began writing while in prison in Toledo, *The Spiritual Canticle, Ascent of Mount Carmel* (or *Dark Night of the Soul*) and *Living Flame of Love*, have a quite extraordinary ease and beauty. All have been translated into English, most recently by Roy Campbell.

Joseph *First century*
Husband of Virgin Mary
Feast days March 19 and May 1

The carpenter from Nazareth, Joseph was betrothed to the **Virgin Mary** at the time of the Annunciation. Joseph's understandable misgivings at finding his fiancée with child were allayed by the appearance of an angel in a dream, and the marriage was celebrated before the Roman census took the couple from Nazareth to Bethlehem, where Mary gave birth to Jesus. Subsequent angelic interventions were also responsible for Joseph's decision to take the family into Egypt, to avoid King Herod's massacre of new-born children, and their return to Nazareth after the death of Herod. The role he plays in searching for the 12-year-old Jesus after the feast of the Passover (*Luke* 2^{42-52}) is the last significant mention of Joseph in the New Testament, and completes the gospel portrait of him as a just, loyal and practical foster-father and husband.

The mid-second-century *Protoevangelium of James* maintains that Joseph was already an old man at the time of the birth of Christ, perhaps because John implies he was dead by the time of the Crucifixion (he speaks of the Virgin Mary being taken into the home of "the disciple whom Jesus loved"), but on the whole this seems unlikely. The medieval cult of Joseph was only widespread in the East, where the fifth- to seventh-century *History of Joseph the Carpenter* enjoyed a large audience. In the West interest was localized, and in the majority of surviving medieval mystery plays Joseph is essentially a figure of fun. The great Counter-Reformation divines, **Ignatius of Loyola** and **Theresa of Ávila**, were principally responsible for the renewal of his cult in southern Europe and its diffusion to the New World. By this date, the emphasis had begun to change, and the promise of comfort to all who act in the name of Joseph, a promise contained in the *History of Joseph the Carpenter*, led to his adoption by innumerable convents and hospitals.

BELOW: *The Holy Family in the Carpenter's Workshop.* Rembrandt's ink and wash drawing of the 1630s shows Joseph bent over his workbench; as in most representations he is depicted at some distance from the Virgin and Child.

RIGHT: *The Presentation in the Temple and the Flight into Egypt.* Joseph is seen as a swarthy Flemish peasant in Melchior Broederlam's stunning painting of 1393-94.

Joseph of Arimathea
First century
Jewish counsellor Feast day March 17

And behold, there was a man named Joseph, a counsellor; and he was a good man, and just: (The same had not consented to the counsel and deed of them;) he was of Arimathea, a city of the Jews; who also himself waited for the kingdom of God. This man went unto Pilate, and begged the body of Jesus. And he took it down, and wrapped it in linen, and laid it in a sepulchre that was hewn in stone, wherein never man before was laid. (*Luke* 23[50-53]).

All four canonical gospels agree that Joseph of Arimathea took Christ down from the cross and laid him in the tomb, John adding that he was "a disciple of Jesus, but secretly for fear of the Jews."

The later accounts are legion. Joseph is given prominence in the fourth-century *Acts of Pilate*, where he is credited with founding the first church at Lydda. The most popular story, in south-west England at least, associates Joseph with the foundation of Glastonbury and the bringing of the Holy Grail to Britain. This first appears in a version of William of Malmesbury's *De Antiquitate Glastoniensis Ecclesiae* (*On the Antiquity of Glastonbury Churches*), probably written about 25 years after the 1191 "discovery" of the body of King Arthur. Here we are told that Joseph was sent from Gaul by Philip the Apostle to bring Christianity to the British, and to ease this task he

was initially buried during the fourth century. If so, he was placed in a rock-cut tomb in the island's highest church, and at the end of a processional way. Gemile was abandoned after it was threatened by an Arab fleet in the mid-seventh century, when it is thought the body of Nicholas was moved to the inland safety of Myra.

Things only began to take on a universal dimension after Methodius, Patriarch of Constantinople between 842 and 847, wrote a life of Nicholas, a text which became known in the West through a tenth-century Latin translation. Methodius' life is a brilliant web of pious fiction, guaranteed to attract a wide following by appealing to just about every disadvantaged group imaginable, and seems to have taken Europe by storm. The principal stories subsequently associated with Nicholas are all to be found here, mostly revolving around threes: the three sailors he saved from a tempest off the coast of Asia Minor; the three unjustly condemned men he released from prison; the three bags of gold he dropped through a poor man's window, to provide his daughters with a dowry and so save them from prostitution (the origin, incidentally, of the three golden balls which act as a pawnbroker's sign); and the three young boys he brought to life after they had been murdered in a brine-tub by an unscrupulous butcher. Sailors, prisoners, children and unmarried women – all began to see in Nicholas a protector.

The emergence of Bari (Apulia, Italy) as the center of the cult is the result of one of the most celebrated cases of reliquary theft of the Middle Ages. By the middle of the eleventh century, Lycia was in the hands of the Saracens and the tomb of Nicholas at Myra was thus technically under Moslem control, although the shrine itself was still served by a community of monks. Despite this latter fact, and partly motivated by news from Venice that the maritime community there was also planning a raid on Myra, 62 sailors in three ships set sail from Bari with the express intention of seizing the body. The raid was successful and on May 9, 1087, Elias, abbot of San Benedetto de Bari, received the relics of St. Nicholas on the quayside. Thereafter Elias began work on a new church to accommodate the saint, and two years later, while Pope Urban II was in Bari, the relics were translated into the crypt of the church of San Nicola.

The pilgrimage to the shrine of San Nicola at Bari was among the most prolific

ABOVE: St. Nicholas in prison, striking late thirteenth-century representation of Nicholas sharing the fate of the prisoners, of whom he was regarded as protector.

LEFT: St. Nicholas resurrects the boys in the brine-tub (Rouen, rue St-Romain). As a protector of children and prostitutes, images of St. Nicholas were frequently attached to the angle-posts of late medieval houses. This particular example dates from the late fifteenth-century, and borrows from a popular fourteenth-century version of the story, which situates the action in Athens and substitutes the two sons of a wealthy merchant for the three students of the earliest account.

of the Middle Ages, and served to further popularize an already popular saint. The number of churches dedicated to Nicholas in western Europe is testimony to this, as is the habit of giving presents to children on the feast of St. Nicholas (December 6), which seems first to have taken hold in the Netherlands during the fifteenth century. A Dutch dialect form of St. Nicholas, *Sinteklaas*, is the origin of Santa Claus, and as the tradition of gifts merged with ancient Norse winter rites in the Dutch colonies of North America, Santa Claus became Father Christmas.

Nicholas the Pilgrim
1075-94
Pilgrim Feast day June 2

A Greek youth, allegedly from Stiro, Nicholas vowed to undertake a pilgrimage to Rome, took ship to Ótranto and wandered up the Apulian coast. He traveled carrying a cross, his speech limited to the words *Kyrie Eleison* (Lord, have mercy), a cry which was taken up by the crowds of children who followed him. As he wound through Lecce, Bríndisi and Bari, he was taken for a lunatic and generally treated as an object of ridicule. He fell ill on reaching Trani, and died on the steps of the cathedral on June 2, 1094. Miracles were reported at the grave within days of his death, and in 1098 Bishop Bisantius took advantage of the gathering of prelates at the council of Bari to have the canonization of Nicholas the Pilgrim rushed through by Pope Urban II. Work on a new cathedral to accommodate the shrine of Nicholas the Pilgrim probably began in the same year, 1098, but it was a slow campaign and the relics were only translated into the crypt in 1143, when the cathedral was rededicated to San Nicola Pellegrino.

Nicholas the Pilgrim is a good example of a cult inspired by rivalry with a neighbor. In 1087, Elias of Bari had taken delivery of the relics of the great eastern Mediterranean miracle-worker, Nicholas of Myra (see **Nicholas**), and Bari was a mere 30 miles along the coast. Trani even seems to have played a part in the struggle for the possession of the relics of Nicholas of Myra after they had arrived. In a number of respects Nicholas the Pilgrim offers an interesting parallel with the later cult of William of Perth (died 1201) at Rochester. Like Rochester, on the road to the shrine of **Thomas Becket** at Canterbury, Trani lay on the route

to a major pilgrimage center, and grew to profit from its position. And although neither cult ever seriously compared with those of Canterbury and Bari, their proven miracle-working powers developed into significant subsidiary attractions.

Olaf *995-1030*
Martyr and patron saint of Norway
Feast day July 29

A son of the noted Norse chieftain Harold Grenske, Olaf converted to Christianity in Normandy. By 1013 he was in England, and supported Ethelred II against the invasion army of Swein Forkbeard, subsequently finding employment with Duke Richard II of Normandy in his 1016 campaign against Odo of Chartres. His military skills were also recognized back home, and after defeating Swein in a naval battle in 1016 he ascended to the throne of Norway. His

ABOVE: St. Nicholas offers three bags of gold to the dowerless daughters, in this seventeenth-century woodcut.

RIGHT: St. Olaf (York; St Olave, Marygate). York was an important tenth-century Viking city and Olaf sustained a strong following there well into the sixteenth century. This stained glass figure dates from *c.*1500 and forms part of the east window.

political methods have much in common with those of his tenth-century predecessor, Olaf Tryggvesson; both of them were happy to coerce the Norse into accepting Christianity and to use any means available to root out heathenism. Olaf was defeated in battle by Cnut in 1028, however, and forced to withdraw to Sweden. His attempt to regain the Norwegian throne during the unpopular reign of Swein, son of Cnut, met with disaster and at the battle of Stiklestad, on July 29, 1030, his army was annihilated and he himself killed.

Olaf was proclaimed a martyr almost immediately. Legends of his asceticism grew, and reports of the healing powers of the waters which flowed from his grave reached Grimkell, Bishop of Nidaros (Trondheim), prompting the good bishop to build a chapel over the site. On August 3, 1031, in a state of apparent incorruption, Olaf's body was solemnly translated into a shrine. The growth of the cult was equally rapid, and the feast was observed throughout most of Scandinavia by the end of the eleventh century, while the earlier chapel was expanded as the cathedral church of Trondheim during the 1180s. His feast is also common to a number of English calendars, and with over 40 ancient church dedications in Britain, concentrated in the older Viking areas, Olaf must be counted one of the more popular saints of medieval northwestern Europe.

BELOW: Trani Cathedral. The bronze doors at Trani were designed by the local metalworker, Barisano de Trani, between 1175 and 1179. They depict, among other subjects, scenes from the life and miracles of St. Nicholas the Pilgrim.

Pantaleon *Died c.304?*
Martyr Feast day July 27

The name Pantaleon translates as "all-merciful," and although no early account of his life survives, the cult was popular in Bithynia (the region south and east of the sea of Marmara) from the fifth century onward. According to a late *Passio*, he was brought up a Christian by his mother, Eubula, but lapsed into paganism before being converted back into the Faith by a Christian named Hermalaos. His career as a medic led to his being appointed physician to the Emperor Galerius. He was denounced as a Christian during the persecution of Diocletian, and beheaded at Nicomedia in 304 or 305. He was widely venerated in the East as a healer and miracle-worker, and in the West as a patron of physicians. The Emperor Justinian was probably responsible for rebuilding his church at Nicomedia (Bithynia), while both Cologne and Ravello were important centers for his cult in the West.

ABOVE: The west front of San Pantaleon, Cologne. As one of the main centers of the cult of San Pantaleon, Cologne acquired a church dedicated to the martyr under Archbishop Bruno, brother of the Emperor Otto II. Work began in 966 and the high altar was dedicated in 980, with the western choir added c.1000.

LEFT: *St. Pantaleon*, miniature from a twelfth-century Cologne gospel book. St. Pantaleon was rumored to be particularly helpful to those suffering from headaches.

Patrick *c.390-c.461*
Apostle of the Irish Feast day March 17

Patrick was born to a Christian Romano-British family who owned property at Bannavem Taburniae (site unidentified, but probably in western England or south-west Scotland). His father, Calpurnius, was a deacon in the Church. According to his own *Confessio*, written in Ireland toward the end of his life, Patrick was enslaved by Irish pirates at the age of 16 and set to work as a herdsman at "Foclut," probably in County Mayo. After six years of servitude he escaped, managed to make his way to a distant port and took ship to a "foreign land." The sequence of events from here is unclear and the subject of much scholarly controversy, but it seems Patrick was trained for the priesthood, returned to his family, and at some point in the early 430s was sent to Ireland as a missionary bishop. A number of discordant traditions about this period developed in the seventh century, many of them recorded in the *Book of Armagh*, according to which he was trained as a monk either at Lérins (Provence) or by **Germanus** at Auxerre (Burgundy). Britain is more likely, although Patrick probably did visit Gaul, and his training was a cause of considerable regret to him in his later life, when he bewailed how unlearned and intellectually ill-equipped he was.

Patrick must have arrived in Ireland shortly after Palladius had left. Palladius was originally sent by Pope Celestine I (422-31) as first Bishop of Ireland and worked in Wicklow, but he found few followers and retired to Scotland where, it is thought, he died. Patrick was probably appointed bishop as Palladius' successor, some time before 435, and established himself in the north, preaching, persuading local chieftains to entrust him with the education of their sons, and baptizing the newly converted. He founded the bishopric of Armagh, which he used as a base for his missionary journeys, and began to organize the Irish Church on the same diocesan principles as obtained in the surviving Roman Empire. It was an extremely successful mission and resulted in the foundation of the earliest monastic communities of monks or nuns in Ireland, as well as a system of suffragan bishoprics, but it was not without problems. He was constantly under threat from chieftains suspicious of the erosion of their authority, and encountered opposition from what appears to be a significant faction

LEFT: *The Devil Tempting St. Patrick* (Parisian engraving of 1530). Like many an early Christian saint, Patrick was prone to visitations from demons and tempters.

BELOW: *St. Patrick*, St. Patrick's Cathedral, New York. Neo-Gothic statue of Patrick as bishop and proselytizer.

within the Church, who saw him as a barely educated halfwit. He addresses this latter charge quite specifically in his *Confessio*, and with great modesty and dignity announces his personal *credo*: "I, Patrick, a sinner, am the most ignorant . . . among the faithful. I owe it to God's Grace that so many people should be born again to him through me."

Only one other text by St. Patrick survives, a letter to the British chieftain Coroticus, protesting about the attacks of British slavers on the Christian congregations of Ireland, and both his date and place of death are unknown. Early in the 460s seems the likely date, but as he was not buried at Armagh, disputes as to the ownership of his relics arose during the Middle Ages. Downpatrick was the most favored candidate, but there were other contenders, and even Glastonbury (Somerset) put forward a claim. The later stories of Patrick expelling the snakes from Ireland, or silencing the druids on the hill of Slane and confronting Laoghaire, "High King of Ireland," are legendary accretions and do not form part of his *Confessio*. Nonetheless the story of the snakes, and of Patrick expounding the nature of the Trinity by comparing it to a shamrock, gave rise to the most popular visualization of St. Patrick, as a preacher surrounded by snakes and shamrock.

Paul *Died c.65* AD
Apostle of the Gentiles.
Feast day June 29

Born at Tarsus in Cilicia to a Jewish family of the tribe of Benjamin, Paul was given the name Saul and raised as a Pharisee, receiving instruction from the renowned Rabbi Gamaliel in Jerusalem. Saul was among the early persecutors of Christianity, guarding the clothes of those who stoned **Stephen** and making "havoc of the church, entering into every house, and hailing men and women [committing] them to prison" (*Acts* 8[3]). It was while he was on his way to

LEFT: St. Paul lowered from the walls of the city of Damascus (Palermo, Capella Palatina), detail from the brilliant mosaics in Roger II's mid-twelfth-century court chapel.

RIGHT: *St. Paul at Ephesus*. Gustave Doré's mid-nineteenth-century engraving represents the burning of the books "of the men which used curious arts" at Ephesus. Having confessed their misdeeds to Paul, they were converted to Christianity.

Damascus to arrest more Christians that he underwent his famous conversion, the story being repeated three times in *Acts of the Apostles*. According to these Saul saw a great light and heard the words:

Saul, Saul, why persecutest thou me? And he said, Who art thou, Lord? And the Lord said, I am Jesus whom thou persecutest: it is hard for thee to kick against the pricks. Arise, and go into the city, and it shall be told thee what thou must do (*Acts* 9⁴⁻⁶).

He was baptized by Ananias and then retired to spend three years in solitude and prayer in Arabia. When he returned to Damascus, the Nabataean king, Aretas, was so hostile that he had to be lowered in a basket from the city walls at the dead of night to make good his escape. He made his way to Jerusalem, where the Christian community was understandably cautious, and it was wholly due to the advocacy of the Apostle Barnabas that doubts were allayed and Saul accepted. Little is known about the period immediately after this, and it was several years later that Barnabas summoned Paul to Antioch, and along with **Mark** they set sail for Cyprus on the first missionary journey. During this voyage Barnabas seems to have ceded his position as leader to Saul, who is first referred to as Paul in *Acts of the*

BELOW: *St. Paul* (Ravenna, Arian Baptistry). In this mosaic of *c.*495, Paul is seen carrying the scrolls of the Law and leading a procession of the Apostles toward the *Crux Splendidior*, or jeweled cross, a reference perhaps to the silver-gilt cross which Theodosius II set up on Golgotha.

pagan family who was secretly raised in the Christian faith by his nurse, Crescentia, and her husband, Modestus. The cult took on a wider appeal after some relics of Vitus were translated to the abbey of Corvey (West-phalia) in 836, where they proved particu-larly useful in curing nervous disorders. As such, Vitus was considered the protector of those suffering from epilepsy, snake-bites, or convulsive fits, a group of which (the family of pathological diseases given the umbrella term *chorea*) became known as St. Vitus' Dance. The cult was strongest in southern Italy, Germany and Bohemia, where the late medieval cathedral at Prague took a dedication to St. Vitus.

Werburgh
Died late seventh century
Abbess Feast day February 3

Werburgh was the daughter of Wulfhere, King of Mercia, and was probably born *c.*650. The contemporary records are silent, and most of what is known is derived from the *Liber Eliensis* and a late-eleventh-century *Vita* written by Goscelin, probably while he was a monk at Canterbury. Accord-ing to these traditions, Werburgh retired to her great-aunt **Etheldreda**'s monastery at Ely after her father died in 670. She spent the rest of what seems a relatively short life establishing new monastic houses in Mercia – Weedon (Northamptonshire), Hanbury (Staffordshire), and Threckingham (Lincolnshire) among them – and died at Threckingham, perhaps as early as 685. Her body was removed to Hanbury for burial, but some time between 893 and 907, Werburgh was translated to the Anglo-Saxon minster at Chester by Aethelflaed, Queen of Mercia.

The fact of this translation suggests that considerable importance was attached to the cult of St. Werburgh, for Aethelflaed's move was part of a broader strategy to establish Chester as an Anglo-Saxon bulwark against the Danes, and is broadly contemporary with her translation of the remains of the Northumbrian king and martyr, Oswald, to Gloucester. The minster was in turn refounded as a Benedictine abbey in 1093, on the advice of **Anselm**, and its dedication to St. Werburgh was retained. Goscelin's *Vita* was probably written to coincide with this refoundation, but despite his use of testimony from Weedon, it is largely legendary. The most celebrated story, Werburgh's resurrection of a goose eaten by a Weedon villager, is a straight borrowing from the life of the eighth-century Flemish nun, Amelburga. Nonetheless the cult of St. Werburgh was sufficiently attractive to persuade the monks at Chester to commission a new shrine in about 1340, whose rare and beautiful base survives in the Lady Chapel of what is now Chester Cathedral.

William of York *Died 1154*
Archbishop Feast day June 8

Born into a noble family related to that of King Stephen, William was known in his own lifetime as William fitz Herbert. He was appointed treasurer to the Chapter of York, perhaps as early as 1130, and chaplain to King Stephen after the latter ascended to the throne in 1135. In 1142 the York Chapter elected William Archbishop of York, following considerable pressure from King Stephen, but the appointment was bitterly opposed by **Bernard of Clairvaux** and the monks at Fountains, who accused William of simony. Theobald, Archbishop of Canterbury, refused to consecrate William, and the dispute was referred to Rome, where Innocent II ruled the appointment valid on condition the accusations leveled by Richard II, abbot of Fountains, were denied on oath by William and the dean of York.

William was finally consecrated archbishop in 1143 by his uncle, Henry of Blois, Bishop of Winchester, and the dispute might have been resolved then and there, but for the dean of York's insistence that his oath should be sworn not by him, but on his behalf. From a Cistercian point of view this was no solution at all, and after Henry Murdac, a personal friend of Bernard of Clairvaux, was appointed abbot of Fountains in 1144, letters were sent to most European prelates denouncing William's consecration as fraudulent. William was summoned to Rome following the election of Pope Eugenius III, a Cistercian, in 1145, and arrived in 1147 to be informed he was suspended. His supporters sacked the abbey of

ABOVE: The St. Werburgh shrine base, from a watercolor by the nineteenth-century English artist Samuel Prout. Between 1635 and 1876 the mid-fourteenth-century base of the shrine of St. Werburgh was incorporated into the bishop's throne, and situated on the south side of the choir of Chester Cathedral. Prout's watercolor of *c*.1847 illustrates the bizarre arrangement which resulted.

Fountains shortly afterward, on which news William was deposed at the Council of Reims and Henry Murdac, his bitter opponent, was consecrated archbishop in his stead. William retreated to Winchester, where he was sheltered by Henry of Blois, joined the monastic priory and led a life of exemplary austerity. Matters only changed in 1153, when Henry Murdac, Bernard of Clairvaux and Pope Eugenius III all died within a few months of each other. Pope Anastasius IV restored William to York, and William in turn promised to recompense Fountains for the damage it had suffered. A month after his 1154 return to York, however, he died suddenly and unexpectedly, quite probably poisoned.

William was buried in the cathedral, where he seems to have become regarded as a martyr, and by the late twelfth century miracles began to be reported at his tomb. He was eventually canonized in 1227, a locally popular cult which answered a definite need, given the tremendous explosion of interest in reliquary cults on the part of thirteenth-century English chapters. Prior to William, all York's sainted archbishops were enshrined elsewhere, John at Beverley, Wilfrid at Ripon, Oswald at Worcester, Paulinus at Rochester. William filled the gap, and was celebrated in the commissioning of a superb new shrine base c.1330, and a justly famous miracle window in 1421.

Wulfstan *c.1009-95*
Bishop Feast day January 19

Born at Long Itchington (Warwickshire) and educated in the monastic schools at Evesham and Peterborough, Wulfstan moved to Worcester c.1034, where he was ordained priest by Bishop Brihteah, and entered the cathedral priory as a monk shortly afterward. Thereafter he served as sacristan and prior until Bishop Aldred's elevation to the archbishopric of York created a vacancy, and Edward the Confessor approved Wulfstan's appointment as Bishop of Worcester in 1062.

Wulfstan's episcopate coincided with the Norman Conquest and the subsequent reform of the English Church. Remarkably for an Anglo-Saxon prelate, and particularly one whose relations with King Harold were such that he negotiated with the Northumbrian earls on his behalf, Wulfstan developed a good working relationship with the new Norman settlers. He openly supported the decrees of the 1075 Council of London,

and though his relations with Lanfranc (Archbishop of Canterbury, 1070-89) were initially complicated by Worcester's historical relationship with York, Wulfstan accepted Lanfranc's ruling that his see was a suffragan of Canterbury. Co-operation between the two became close during the late 1070s, and together they should be given the credit for extinguishing the Anglo-Irish slave trade. His administration of the diocese was also much admired by Lanfranc, who noted the enthusiasm with which he encouraged the foundation of new parish churches, assiduously visited all areas under his control, and bravely attempted to enforce clerical celibacy.

Although he shed tears at the demolition of the Anglo-Saxon church, Wulfstan approved the building of a new cathedral at Worcester in 1084, whose choir was sufficiently advanced for the monks to take up residence in 1089. His presidency of a synod in the crypt of this church in 1092 was the last major event in Wulfstan's life, and in 1095, by then in his eighties and one of the very last Anglo-Saxon-born churchmen to hold high office, he died. He was buried in his new cathedral, and within a few years the first cures were reported at his tomb. This tomb was described by William of Malmesbury, writing in the 1120s: "It lies between two *piramides* vaulted over above with a beautiful stone arch. A wooden beam projects out above, which has fixed in it iron grills, which are called spiders' webs." Wulfstan's formal canonization only took place in 1203, but the cult was popular from the time of his death, and remained so until the destruction of the shrine by Henry VIII's commissioners in 1538.

BELOW: King John's tomb (Worcester Cathedral). In 1232 King John was placed in a new sarcophagus in front of the main altar of Worcester Cathedral and close to the shrines of Wulfstan and Oswald. The position was prestigious, to say the least, but even more startlingly, images of two bishops, Wulfstan and Oswald again, were carved to either side of John's head, commending the dead king to God. The detail chosen here illustrates one of the two sained bishops (which is Wulfstan and which Oswald is unclear) with John's head to the left.

Acknowledgments

The publisher would like to thank designer David Eldred. We should also like to thank the following institutions, agencies and individuals for supplying photographic material.

AA Photo Library: page 46
AKG, London: page 32
Courtesy of the Benedictine Convent of St. Hildegard, Rudesheim-Eibingen: page 76
Bettmann Archive, New York: pages 4, 7, 11 both, 15 both, 16 both, 17, 25 top, 27, 30, 34 bottom, 36, 37, 38, 39 top, 40, 42 top, 45, 48, 50, 51, 52, 53 top, 57, 61, 64, 66, 70, 71, 74, 75 all, 80, 82, 84, 85, 91 top, 94, 100 both, 104, 106, 107, 110, 112, 114 both, 121 both, 122, 126, 127 top, 128, 130 bottom, 131 top, 133, 137 bottom, 143, 146, 149, 152, 155 top, 156 top
Bibliothèque Municipale, Poitiers: page 138
The Board of Trinity College, Dunblin: page 12
British Library, London: pages 3, 10, 59, 124, 153, 156 bottom
British Museum, London: page 98
Cartuja de Miraflores, Burgos: 79
Courtesy of the Conservateur des Antiquités et Objets d'Art, St-Julien Cathedral, Le Mans: page 72 both
The Dean and Chapter of Durham Cathedral: page 42 bottom
Courtesy of the Dean and Chapter of Westminster: page 135
Giraudon, Paris: page 77
Haskins, Susan: page 120 top
Life File, London: pages 13 (photo Andrew Ward), 31 (photo Terry O'Brien), 69 bottom (photo Emma Lee), 123 (photo Andrew Ward), 157 (Photo Emma Lee), 159 (by kind permission of the Dean and Chapter, Worcester, photo Terry O'Brien)
McCleneghan, Daniel: page 131 bottom
Mackenchnie-Jarvis, Mr. J.P.: page 14
McNeill, John: pages 9 bottom left, 18 bottom, 87, 115, 127 bottom, 129 right, 130 top, 139, 154 top
MAS, Barcelona: pages 81, 96, 125
The Master and Fellows of Corpus Christi College, Cambridge: page 24
The Master and Fellows of University College, Oxford: page 44
Musée de l'Abbaye St-Germain, Auxerre/Cliché Hervé: page 144
Musée des Beaux-Arts, Dijon: page 99
Musées departementaux de la Seine-Maritime, photo François Dugue: page 94 top
National Gallery, London: pages 1, 26, 29 bottom, 35, 55, 60 bottom, 73, 92, 93, 141, 142, 148
Courtesy Pélérinage Sainte Thérèse de Lisieux: page 147
Photo Resources, Canterbury, Kent: pages 6, 9 top and bottom right, 18 top, 29 top, 34 top, 39 bottom, 53 bottom, 54, 60 top, 66, 88, 90, 95 bottom, 108, 109 top, 120 bottom, 129 left, 132, 134, 137 top
Private Collection, Gloucestershire, photo Nick Nicholson: page 56
Reproduced by permission of Cheshire County Council Archives and Local Studies Service: page 158
Scala, Florence: 2, 19, 20/21, 22/23, 25 bottom, 41, 43, 58, 62/63, 68-69, 86, 102, 105, 109 bottom, 111, 113, 116, 117, 136, 140, 145, 150/151, 154/155
Sonia Halliday Photographs: 49, 97, 103
Städelsches Kunstinstitut, Frankfurt: page 28
Szépmüvézeti Museum, Budapest: page 83